NAUTICAL QUARTERLY

SPRING 1983

PUBLISHER: DONALD McGRAW, JR.
EDITOR: JOSEPH GRIBBINS
DESIGNER: MARILYN ROSE
MANAGING EDITOR: MICHAEL LEVITT
ASSOCIATE EDITOR: REBECCA SMITH
DESIGN ASSISTANT: RAFAEL RIVERA

MANAGING DIRECTOR: C.S. LOVELACE
CIRCULATION DIRECTOR: DAVID B. WALLACE
CIRCULATION MANAGER: JOHN M. CORNWALL
OFFICE MANAGER: LIZ MONTALVO
SPECIAL PROJECTS: MIRANDA SCHILLER
ASSISTANT TO THE PUBLISHER: LAURA RIEGEL

CONTRIBUTING EDITORS:
H. D. "KNOTS" NESBITT/THE WEST COAST
ANGUS LENNOX/THE U.K.
ANNICA DAHLSTROM/SCANDINAVIA
MAXIM GOLIARD/THE CONTINENT
T. FREMANTLE FONG/THE FAR EAST

CANTIERI RIVA—AN EXCELLENCE ALL ITS OWN	STANLEY ROSENFELD	2
MONTECARLO 66		14
IMAGES OF THE PAN AM CLIPPER CUP	MICHAEL LEVITT	18
72 YEARS OF YACHT RACING	ARTHUR KNAPP, JR.	30
DAISY	STAN GRAYSON	48
PHILIP C. BOLGER, BOAT DESIGNER, GLOUCESTER, MASSACHUSETTS	JOSEPH GRIBBINS	58
FOOLS RUSH IN WHERE ANGLERS FEAR TO TREAD	DAVID FINKELSTEIN AND JACK LONDON	80
DER MINI-ZWÖLFER—A SMALL BOAT BEGINS A LONG JOURNEY	PETER NEUMANN	90
SHANNON 50 KETCH—A SURVEY	FRASER AND JEAN FRASER-HARRIS	98
NAUTICAT 52—A SURVEY	FRASER AND JEAN FRASER-HARRIS	102
THE MARINE ENGINE: ITS HISTORY	DONALD B. SHARP	106
LETTERS		118
CREDITS		120

NAUTICAL QUARTERLY IS PUBLISHED IN WINTER, SPRING, SUMMER AND FALL BY NAUTICAL QUARTERLY CO., 373 PARK AVENUE SOUTH, NEW YORK, N.Y. 10016. COPYRIGHT ©1983 NAUTICAL QUARTERLY CO.: ALL RIGHTS RESERVED UNDER PAN AMERICAN AND UNIVERSAL COPYRIGHT CONVENTIONS: REPRODUCTION WITHOUT PERMISSION IS PROHIBITED. EDITORIAL SUBMISSIONS SHOULD BE SENT TO THE ADDRESS ABOVE, AND SHOULD BE ACCOMPANIED BY A SELF-ADDRESSED, STAMPED ENVELOPE. WE WILL ACCEPT NO RESPONSIBILITY, HOWEVER, FOR UNSOLICITED GRAPHIC OR EDITORIAL MATERIAL. ON EDITORIAL MATTERS, PHONE 212-685-9114. SUBSCRIPTION CORRESPONDENCE, BOOKSTORE ORDERS AND ORDERS FOR BACK COPIES SHOULD BE SENT TO THE ADDRESS ABOVE, OR BY PHONE TO 212-685-9114. FOR INQUIRIES OR COMPLAINTS ABOUT SUBSCRIPTIONS, PHONE 212-685-9114. U.S. AND CANADIAN SUBSCRIPTIONS ARE $60 PER YEAR. ALL OTHERS ARE $66 (U.S.). FOREIGN SUBSCRIBERS ARE SERVED ONLY BY SURFACE MAIL. SECOND-CLASS POSTAGE FOR NAUTICAL QUARTERLY (ISSN 0199-0837) IS PAID AT NEW YORK, N.Y. AND AT ADDITIONAL MAILING OFFICES.

CANTIERI
Riva

BY STANLEY ROSENFELD

—AN EXCELLENCE ALL ITS OWN

When Gino Gervasoni, President of Cantieri Riva, rummages through his office portfolio of family photographs, there is a story to be told about every one. Signor Gervasoni's office is big, as stunningly decorated as his boats and, through a wall of windows, surveys the Lake of Iseo and the mountains beyond. It is a presidential office suited to one of the great yachtbuilders of the world. When Gino Gervasoni talks about his business he can be very serious; but when he tells the stories of the old photographs his face lights up with a delightful little smile, first his lips, then his cheeks and then—for emphasis—he tilts his head. In moments, there is a pixie quality in his expression, and there is a little pixie quality in some of his stories, too. □ Gervasoni's photographs show kings, princes and movie stars in remarkable profusion. One photograph shows a distinguished-looking young man in a flowing burnous standing with his hand on a gleaming Riva Aquarama. He had come to the shipyard unannounced and, through his interpreter, soon communicated that he had come to buy. He was shown through the plant, and with a catalog in hand he pointed to six boats and let it be known that he wanted to purchase all six. Then he indicated that he wanted to purchase a Rolls-Royce and a Ferrari. There is a great deal of image identification among Riva, Rolls-Royce and Ferrari visible in the Riva reception room. When the Rolls and Ferrari dealers arrived, the gentleman ordered two Rolls-Royce (Rolls-Royce is always singular) and two Ferraris in the same manner he had ordered the six Rivas.

On page 3, Gino Gervasoni's face lights up with characteristic amusement as he sits in his enormous office with its panoramic view of Lago d'Iseo. Out on the lake, there is plenty to see, from the whimsical castle of a summer place shown on page 2, to the contrasting modernism of the Riva plant's waterfront. In the dozen buildings of the complex, Riva's assembly line blends modern machinery and efficiency with hand craftsmanship not only in rare woods but in metal and fiberglass, producing powerboats whose polish and perfection are legend. A spirited example is the Riva 2000 shown here, a 36′ projectile driven by three 350-hp V8 engines to speeds of 50 knots.

Above, Ernesto Riva, of the second generation of Riva boatbuilders, the man who per- suaded his father to build the small yard shown here on the lake. His son Serafino, shown at far left in the festive boat below, and at right above with his son Carlo, carried on the business from 1907 to 1945.

When Riva yachts leave the lake, they are delivered to princes, potentates, politicians, movie stars, tycoons, and distinguished ordinary people who can afford them...

Several days later a letter arrived with proper credit and shipping instructions to a Persian Gulf emirate, with the information that the Rivas and the autos were to be placed in a new showroom which would be completed before their arrival. The merchandise was efficiently paid for and shipped, and nothing more was heard from the Persian Gulf port for a year. Then the gentleman returned to Riva. He had come to buy some more new Rivas, Rolls-Royce and Ferraris. When asked—in hope of improving the dealer relationship—how the previously shipped units had been displayed in the new showroom there was a moment of silence. It turned out that neither the Rivas, the several Rolls-Royce nor the Ferraris had ever been in the showroom. They were unable to use the showroom. The showroom, they explained, had been built on a pool of oil and, when completed, suffered from a continuous seepage of oil through the showroom floor that no one had been able to stop. But, they said with a smile, they hoped that by the time a new shipment arrived someone would find a solution to the nuisance.

When Gervasoni tells this story his face lights up in such a way that a listener is not quite sure whether he is pleased with the effectiveness of his catalog as a sales tool or amused by the oil on the showroom floor. The catalog is something special.

The photographs in sunlit color on some of Europe's best printing paper show all eleven Riva models, from the 19' Rudy Super to the 66' Montecarlo, and they show the boats' "prendisoli" utilized in classic Italian fashion, with lovely ladies in mini-bikinis sunbathing. The noun "prendisole" (literally, take the sun), is not specific. A dictionary definition is sunsuit, but in common usage the word can mean a sunwashed terrace or a bath towel on a beach. Riva's boats provide the ne plus ultra of "prendisole," a spiritual as well as physical place under the sun, aboard what many consider the ultimate modern motor yacht.

Riva yachts are built at Sarnico on Lago d'Iseo, a picturebook lake of misty blue water, dancing reflections, enchanted little islands, and turreted castles of boathouses and summer places. Sometimes a patient lone fisherman in a long, narrow boat stands under his big hat with a long pole in hand and lifts a glistening fish aboard. Little villages dot the shore, rugged mountain peaks loom beyond.

The yachts are built in a remarkably orderly plant equipped with the best of tools, technology and materials, by white-coated men who have a strong, traditional feeling for craftsmanship. The work is done in an environment filled with soft light, clean air, ample space and evident good fellowship, under a management dedicated to the quality and subtle aesthetics of the product and the joy their clients can find in its use. When Riva yachts leave the lake, they are delivered to princes, potentates, politicians, movie stars, tycoons and distinguished ordinary people who can afford them and who richly enjoy them. If this description seems like a Walt Disney plot for a movie that might be called "Riva in Wonderland," the only wonder is that it is all real.

For one thing, it seems strange to build 60' motor yachts on a little lake miles away from access to the sea or any coastal port. But it is possible for Riva to plan even a 72-footer because they have built a remarkable transport to carry their big yachts to the sea. The huge steel structure carries a boat neatly cradled inside with its keel just inches off the ground. The amazing thing rests at either end on what looks like a 56-wheel dolly, each dolly with its own 10-wheel truck for propulsion and guidance. The trip to either Genoa or Venice over secondary roads is slow, made possible at all by the straightening of hard curves, the demolition of walls and the dismantling and reassembly of cables along the way.

Some Rivas are shipped by air. There is a photograph that shows a 37', 50-knot Riva 2000 powered by three 350-hp engines on the tarmac alongside a Transmeridian cargo plane for air shipment to the Shah of Iran. On another occasion a German industrialist phoned in to have the builder tell him how long it would take to fly a boat to him in Acapulco. When he found it could be done in a week, he said, "Great, ship it out." He was entertaining an interesting young woman and he felt that, after a week, he should provide something new and stimulating for their vacation.

Whether moored in Qatar, Hong Kong, Monte Carlo or Fort Lauderdale, a Riva is new and stimulating in design and workmanship. However, with the single exception of the biggest in the line, the 66' Montecarlo, Riva yachts are not custom built. It is a Riva principle that an owner should not have to waste time outfitting a new yacht or searching for an accessory. Standard equipment on the 50' Superamerica lists 226 items including stereo, VHF radiotelephone, depth sounder, barometer, hygrometer, thermometer, quartz watch, air-conditioning, table linen, tableware, crystal glasses, bedsheets, Riva T-shirts and a beach towel. Radar and Satnav are standard on the bigger yachts.

As Luciano Greggio, assistant to the president, says: "If a customer is looking for a different color or different curtains, we say, 'Sorry, this is the boat. Our designers and architects think this is the best solution, the best compromise; but if you do want something different, please go ahead and have the curtains replaced.'"

"Our clientele," says Greggio, "is very rich, very sophisticated, living at the very, very top of the social scale. He doesn't want to take delivery of a boat and then go to a dealer who specializes in marine equipment to have radar mounted and satellite mounted. He wants the warranty that everything on the boat is from Riva, so we give the boat complete—completely decorated—everything."

Few yacht yards have been building so continuously
for more than a hundred years, and very few with management handed down from
father to son, or to son-in-law.

The reasoning behind Riva's standard yacht and Henry Ford's notions of the standard Model T are worlds apart. Henry Ford standardized to make a simple, inexpensive vehicle for the masses. Riva standardizes to make an exquisitely luxurious and ultra-special yacht for a wealthy few. Riva's customer surveys show that a typical owner spends three, at most four weeks per year aboard his yacht. Riva plans its products to have all of the pleasures and none of the problems, so that owners can savor every minute of every day aboard without a care.

To more readily understand the Riva business philosophy of technology in perfect service to pleasure, you must, perhaps, understand its roots in Italian history and culture. The Protestant work ethic never really took hold in Italy, despite the geographic proximity of Calvin and Luther. For centuries, artists and artisans have cherished the opportunity to work in Italy. This ancient place of Etruscan, Greek, Roman and European Renaissance success, seems to have a special quality of climate and light, as well as the inspiration drawn from great works of genius. Italy affords

rich food for the creative urge. But along with the beauty are signs of struggle and of the inevitable toll of corruption. Though singing is often heard in the streets, there is a strong streak of cynicism in the Italian temperament. It seems appropriate, on the one hand, to be skeptical, particularly toward authority, and on the other to savor the pleasures of the moment, of which there can be many.

Italy is also the land where Pliny the Younger about the year 100 A.D. wrote of "that indolent but agreeable condition of doing nothing." *Dolce far niente,* it became, or "sweet doing nothing." Sitting at a sidewalk cafe, sipping coffee and watching the world go by is one familiar evidence of sweet doing nothing. Another, for most Italians, is luxuriating on a towel under the sun, the sweetest of Mediterranean sweetnesses. Italians are a theatrical people. If body language can tell a story, then in Italy the beach towel becomes a stage, the sun becomes the great spotlight from above. The body, reclining in sweet repose, seems with no external evidence to be singing soaring arias. Italians do not just take the sun, they consume it. Each in his own way, under the spotlight from the sky, creates an inward moment of ecstasy. That is why every Riva, even the little 19′ Rudy Super, has a full-length "prendisole." It is what a proper Italian yachtsman deserves, and fortunately for Riva's sales, it is eagerly bought by a sheik from Kuwait, a tycoon from Hamburg, even a successful realtor from Chicago. Riva's boats are creatures of two Italian traditions—perfect workmanship, a pleasure in itself, and the *dolce far niente* awareness that life is short—but sweet—and that you had better get the sweetness while you can.

Riva's boats were not always so sumptuous. About 1880, Pietro Riva moved from the Oglio river to a modest little shop very near its present location on the shore of the lake. Riva has been building boats there ever since, interrupted only by two World Wars and, in 1969, by one very significant labor strike. Few yacht yards have been building so continuously for more than a hundred years, and very few with management handed down from father to son or, as in this present Riva generation, to son-in-law. Riva has been lucky enough, or wise enough in times of stressful change or disaster, to have new, capable leadership rise from within the family. When it became evident that inadequate facilities in Pietro Riva's first yard on the Oglio river were hindering the yard's growth, his son Ernesto, with aggressive foresight, persuaded Pietro to relocate on the more suitable shore of Lago d'Iseo.

The new yard continued to build two-oared and four-oared boats; but in a new, big shed steam-powered cargo and passenger vessels were built for use on the lake. In the photo files of the yard there is a lovely vignetted photograph of a passenger and cargo boat, perhaps 50′ long, smokestack

Ready for delivery to a customer somewhere in the world, a new Superamerica 50 is shown here on Lago d'Iseo with a Riva workman aboard. It is company policy to test each boat thoroughly three times—at the engine-installation stage, when the boat comes off the assembly line completed, and finally just before delivery, often with the owner aboard. The Superamerica—which has developed through 42′, 45′ and 48′ versions to its current state of perfection as a 50-footer—is a 30-knot motor yacht with twin 400-hp diesels and with sumptuous quarters for an owner's party of four to six and a crew of two. Her current price is $465,000 delivered in Italy, $537,200 delivered in Fort Lauderdale. Riva's eleven models range from the 18′ Rudy Super skiboat to the 66′ Montecarlo shown in these pages, and there are two new boats for 1983.

> Rivas became objects of prestige in the fashionable harbors of the Cote d'Azur, along with the Bugattis, Hispano-Suizas, and Rolls-Royce automobiles that cruised the coast roads.

rakishly tilted aft, docked in front of the shipyard. The photograph, dated 1900, gives some insight into how the business flourished. Ernesto had built a somewhat similar cargo and passenger vessel on order. It turned out to be so successful for its owner that the younger Riva decided to build one for his own use. By this time the staff of the yard had grown, and Ernesto's wife Carolina presided over a kitchen and small eating place where the workmen could have lunch on the premises. Small businesses in Italy are often like families. Carolina noted with interest the tourists sailing by in Ernesto's passenger boat. She realized that tourists must have lunch, too, so with proper empire-building acumen she had the eating space enlarged to accommodate tourists.

In the photograph, the building shed of the yard is to the left. Painted in bold letters under the eaves is the word *Cantiere,* shipyard. Under the eaves of the building in the middle of the photo there is just as boldly painted *Trattoria Del Cantiere,* restaurant of the shipyard. In even bolder type, on the side of Ernesto's sightseeing and cargo boat are the words *Alla Trattoria Del Cantiere,* to the restaurant of the shipyard. The source of information about the Riva trattoria, an article in Gino Gervasoni's Symbol magazine, describes it most attractively: "The small eating place was, indeed, transformed into a beautiful trattoria, where tourists could eat the best fish from the lake, duck and hare, rabbit and polenta, and homemade tagliatelle and gnocchi, all served with genuine local wines. On Sundays, there was even a small organ that played and young people danced, while the old chatted; strangers talked about boats, occasionally even placing some orders." Even in the year 1900, acquiring a Riva could be a sensuous delight.

In May, 1907, disaster struck. During the launching of one of the bigger boats the poppets slipped, the hull fell over and Ernesto Riva, caught underneath, was killed. Within a few days Ernesto's son Serafino carried on. Serafino proved to be responsive to the changing times. It was possible in a small boat, powered with one of the new internal combustion engines, to charge along at thrilling speed. Serafino loved to tinker with and race the small speedboats, so Riva's product became beautifully built small racing boats and fast runabouts until production stopped with World War I.

The yard was slow to return to production after the war, although skilled boatbuilders drifted back, wood could be found for building and there were engines to be had. The airplane industry had developed big ones, and the new motor-car industry built smaller ones, but Serafino Riva was most fascinated by the outboard motor. There is a photograph in the Riva files taken at an outboard race in Venice in the 1930s. Serafino is squatting on his knees, the classic outboard driver's position, in the first Riva outboard competition hull. On the transom of the little boat is a four-cylinder Elto Quad. Beyond the outboard is a four-oared rowing shell. Just beyond the shell, three gondoliers in their gondolas have come out to watch the racers. The motorboat had come to Venice, and its wakes have never stopped splashing the walls of the old palazzi since.

The period between World War I and World War II, the Roaring Twenties, and for Riva the Racing Thirties, was a time of steady growth. The raceboats and gentleman's speedboats the Riva family built were extremely successful. Rivas were acclaimed for their speed and lauded for their quality. They became objects of prestige in the fashionable harbors on the Cote d'Azur, along with the Bugattis, Hispano-Suizas, and Rolls-Royce automobiles that cruised the coast roads. In 1940, war again shut down the plant.

After the ravages of the second World War, Serafino was reluctant to reopen the yard. His 22-year-old-son Carlo, however, was eager to take up the reins. Serafino agreed, but Carlo had to raise the money to take control. It was a difficult time for fundraising, and Carlo found that the banks he approached were no help at all. After many disappointments Carlo joined forces with a boyhood friend, Gino Gervasoni, who sought out Riva's prewar friends, the racing drivers and owners of the 1920s and 1930s, with energy and enthusiasm. Gino raised enough capital to start production, and Carlo applied himself to the production of boats that were works of art. Carlo was a perfectionist, and for the next few years they built only two exquisite runabouts a month. It was a hand-to-mouth existence, but the shipyard kept working and Riva's fame kept growing.

In 1951, Carlo Riva went to the United States to look over boatbuilding methods, but more importantly to secure a dependable supply of American engines. Engines were Riva's biggest production problem, both their financing and the cost of converting them to marine use. Carlo bought a few Chris-Craft engines and was successful in arranging the financing to assure Riva a steady supply. So began another new phase in Riva's development. In a few years Riva switched to Gray engines, then to Chrysler. Early in the 1960s Riva made an arrangement with Thermoelectric in the United States to get Chevrolet Corvette blocks partially adapted to marine use.

Carlo Riva began to effect small changes in the new engines to fit them more exactly to Riva's concept of a no-problem product. He ordered new engine mounts of chrome-plated bronze with chromed brass fittings. Mufflers and exhaust pipes were made of copper and stainless steel. Gasoline and water filters were Inox (stainless steel), and water pumps were bronze. Because of their extensive adaptations on the engines, the Riva plant was authorized to call them Rivas. Today they have the Riva insignia attached and are painted an eye-catching Riva blue.

The 1950s were boom times for Riva. The Riviera was the playground of kings, sultans and a jet set that could well afford exquisite speedboats.

> One aspect of the Riva philosophy can only be
> appreciated after spending a day in the plant—a subtle sense of concern for
> the professional integrity and the well-being of the workers.

Marinas along the Cote d'Azur glowed with the deep brilliance of mahogany under Riva's impeccable eight coats of varnish, and what became the characteristic small pleasure boats of the Med were moored one alongside another like Toyotas in a modern supermarket parking lot. But if the playboys of the Riviera thought that life would never change, the production men at Sarnico knew that change was all around them.

In 1954, Riva switched from their carefully matched Honduras mahogany planking to plywood. It was not just ordinary plywood. Riva, in collaboration with Lodi, began plywood manufacture keeping in mind the very particular qualities they were building into their hulls. They have been working together most successfully ever since. Lodi can form the entire side of the 29′ Super Aquarama in one beautifully matched unit, molded to shape. It takes nearly five days to mold a set of Aquarama topsides in a blending of wood that will be exalted by coats of varnish. That makes for no production problem now, as only about 20 Super Aquaramas are scheduled for this year's production. In the 1960s, however, before the big boat era, at a time when the most Aquaramas per year were being produced, Lodi worked seven days a week to keep up with Riva's assembly line.

The transition from planking stock to plywood which kept all the aesthetic qualities of rare wood took place with almost no visible sign. The advent of fiberglass as a construction material, however, brought dramatic changes in design, model size, sales planning, and just about every aspect of Riva's business other than a commitment to excellence. The changes were not due to fiberglass alone. The late 1960s was a period of heated struggle in Italy between the labor unions and management. By 1969, the conflict came to Riva, and for the first time there was a strike at the plant.

Carlo Riva's reaction was immediate and inwardly consuming. To quote Luciano Greggio: "Carlo Riva was like a father to many people living here in Sarnico. He built, for instance, the walk in front of the lake, and the big lamps on the boardwalk were designed by him. In a way he considered himself a patriarch. When they had the first strike he felt betrayed. All of a sudden he decided to look for a big company who was interested…" Within weeks, Carlo Riva was talking with the Whittaker Corporation, and very soon afterwards the esteemed boatbuilder of Sarnico, Italy, became a part of Whittaker Corporation, based in Los Angeles, California. Carlo Riva stayed on at the yard for a year.

In 1969, a new factory was added for fiberglass production. Wooden construction slowed down. There were about eighty units in wood complete, divided among the four models then building—Aquarama, Ariston, Olympic and Junior. Production on the Ariston was dropped, and the Riva Junior formed the mold for the present Rudy Super, a fiberglass 20-footer priced at about $30,000, f.o.b., Sarnico. Two Riva models are still crafted in wood, the 20.2′ Olympic and the famed 29′ Aquarama Special powered by two 350-hp engines. At more than $100,000, the Riva Aquarama is a collector's item even before it leaves the shipyard.

The fall of 1969 was a troubled time for Riva. Fiberglass construction had brought a new technology. The aftermath of the strike had threatened old associations. The sale of the company implied the promise as well as the uncertainty inherent in new ownership. The management at Riva chose to ignore the possible new problems of overseas ownership and began vigorously to explore the potential available to them. To test the cruiser market they built two fiberglass boats, the 20′ Bahia Mar and the 25′ Sportfisherman, both based on Bertram Yacht's boats of the same name. (Bertram was another property of Riva's new parent company.) They added a few refinements, but at the plant these boats were not felt to be Rivas, as they were not developed by the Riva technical staff. Florida boats, developed for another place and perhaps another style, they just did not feel natural to Riva's Italian style and design concepts.

The first model of the Superamerica, a 42′ boat launched in 1972, was the first completely Riva cruiser in fiberglass, although it followed the Ray Hunt/Bertram example in hull design. Riva will adapt successful ideas from elsewhere, but this yard on one of Italy's loveliest lakes designs and builds according to its own standards and marketing philosophy. When Riva mentions standards they usually say "our high standards." Standards are not specifically listed in their literature, but there is frequent reference to the quality of materials, installation, design, styling, environment, dependability, ease of maintenance and efficient service to owners.

This builder's marketing philosophy can be judged to include dealer relations, production schedules, price, and anticipation of market demand. Overlapping in the areas of standards and marketing philosophy is a very keen awareness of, and a dedication to satisfy, the lifestyle of their wealthy and sophisticated owners. One aspect of the Riva philosophy can only be appreciated after spending a day in the plant—a subtle sense of concern for the professional integrity and the well-being of the workers. After a few hours spent with them, the designation "workers" seems somehow inappropriate. "Gentlemen artisans" seems more correct. Throughout Italy, particularly in small workshops, there are still a large number of master artisans who have a particularly satisfying relationship to their work. One of the joys of visiting Rome is to walk through the old city to watch local artisans at work with leather, wood, wrought iron or marble. They are craftsmen whose work and their joy in it are the meaning of their lives. One senses the same attitude in the Riva plant, and working conditions are far superior there. In the United States there is a new dialogue in the auto industry between management and labor, aimed at convincing the work force that management really wants a good job done, that speed is not everything. There is no question about this in the Riva plant. In every department it is obvious that an impeccable job is everyone's concern.

The introduction of the Superamerica marked a giant step forward for Riva. The decision to build the Superamerica was built on two considerations: first, that there was a market ready to buy a new big Riva motoryacht and, second, that owners of the Riva Aquarama would trade up to a bigger new Riva. These hopes proved right on both counts. Not only was there a market ready and waiting for Riva's new motoryacht but, with the coming of OPEC, new clients flew in from the Persian Gulf area with the regularity if not the frequency of supertankers clearing the Straits of Hormuz. Riva's people were right, too, about the probability that Aquarama owners would move up to the bigger Superamerica. In the years following 1972, as the Superamerica was redesigned from a 42-footer to a 45, a 48 and the present 50′ version, some owners kept trading up. Between 1972 and this writing, 165 Superamericas were built, one complete superyacht every three weeks.

Early in the 1970s a charming gentleman from Lebanon arrived at the plant to look at the Superamerica. He said he was concerned with conditions in Lebanon and thought that it would be wise to invest in a motoryacht he could live aboard if he so chose. He liked the boat and ordered one. Every Riva is tested three times, the first when the engines are installed, usually a three-hour underway test. When the boat is finished and completely decorated it is taken out again so that everything aboard, from the sanitation system to the radar, is checked out. Then, at the time of delivery, the boat is tested again. This is called the customer test, for often the customer goes along. It is generally the most severe test run of all.

The gentleman from Lebanon, his wife and dog came along for the customer test run, and in the course of the day he found himself delighted with the charm of Lago d'Iseo. He took delivery, moved aboard, decorated the boat in native style with hanging rugs and swaying incense burners, and began a cruise around the lake. This was a little lake cruise that lasted three months and brought the Lebanese visitors a lasting delight in things Italian, with emphasis on the trattorias. After the longest shakedown cruise on record at Sarnico, the boat was finally trucked to Venice as a jumping-off port for the cruise back to Lebanon. Venice also proved to have an irresistible number of trattorias and other wonders, as did each port along the way as they inched slowly south. Every few months the people at the Riva plant would hear stories about the remarkably slow but joyful progress their Superamerica was making. When last heard from years later, the boat had passed from the Adriatic to the Ionian Sea, but there was very little easting to be reported in its log.

Which probably proves that a statistical report has room for an exception, and if the average Superamerica owner spends something like three weeks of the year aboard, at least one finds it a year-round home—enroute, of course.

Introduced in 1950, the Riva Aquarama became the classic Mediterranean motorboat in the 'fifties, a status it still enjoys, with gleaming fleets of these boats on the waterfronts of places like Monte Carlo. The Aquarama Special, a 29-footer with twin 350-hp V8 engines, is the current version, shown here. Riva calls her "a precious mahogany sculpture." She's also a useful day boat, with seats for seven passengers, a bed-sized *prendisole*, a swimming platform on the stern, and a berth under the foredeck. The price of a new Aquarama Special is now more than $100,000. But it's an investment; these boats always appreciate in value, and older examples are collected like vintage Ferraris.

MONTECARLO 66

This largest of Riva's dozen boats is firmly in the Italian tradition of fast motor yachts finished and furnished like Riviera apartments—with one exception. As Stanley Rosenfeld explains, this is a thoroughly equipped stock boat— from the Riva tableware in the galley drawers, to the velvet cushions on the L-shaped lounge in the pilothouse, to the dinghy davits on the stern. What you see here is what you get, for a price of about $3 million, delivered, say, in Fort Lauderdale.

The customary Italian approach to a luxury yacht like this one involves the advice of an owner's hired decorators, engineers and other experts who will transform a builder's stock hull into the *padrone*'s personal statement, from drapes to drive train. Riva prefers to deliver a ready-to-go product, meticulously prepared by its own experts. The attitude is autocra-

As the largest of the Rivas, the 66 is "custom built" in the sense that an owner is given some latitude in decor, arrangement and equipment, but Riva still delivers the 66 as a thoroughly tested and equipped boat, ready-to-cruise. Three of these have been built.

tic, but Riva seems to have earned it. One look at these few photos will show the Montecarlo 66 to be a highly civilized cruising machine for an owner's party of six, plus two crew, and it would be an autocratic customer indeed who might want this or that changed.

Only three of these boats have been built since 1981, their first year, and there are none in the United States. The low-deadrise, modified-vee hull and the deck molding are fiberglass; the house structure is aluminum; and standard power is a pair of 12V-71TI Detroit Diesels prepared by Johnson & Towers and rated for 726 hp each. Top speed is 21 knots, a respectable pace for a vehicle whose all-up weight is 40 tons. Cruising speed is 19 knots, and range at this pace is 20 hours of running with 6000 liters of fuel in the tanks.

From the all-important *prendisole* on the foredeck to the afterdeck-with-dining-table, the Montecarlo 66 is distinguished by a cool atmosphere of what Riva describes as "modern and refined solutions, making use of costly materials, marble, leather and prized woods." Unlike many Italian motor yachts, and a few of Riva's, the interior spaces in the 66 are rich but subdued, full of earth tones and natural materials rather than chrome and plastic razzle-dazzle. The flush deck has a pilothouse forward, galley and well-cushioned salon amidships, dining space with wet bar and six-place table aft, and a sheltered afterdeck with another table that serves as the vessel's own open-air café. Below decks are a big locker in the forepeak, crew quarters for two forward, a pair of guest staterooms with head/shower compartments, and amidships a spectacular owner's stateroom with a double bed, large head/shower compartment, and separate dressing room and desk space. The owner's cabin has its own companionway from the

salon; a second companionway to quarters forward is in the pilothouse. More than a third of the after part of the hull is engine and machinery space.

Yachts like this are designed as much for entertaining as for spirited runs to Capri to swim in the sea caves, and the Montecarlo 66 has no fewer than four separate places in which to lounge around drinking iced vermouth and telling stories—six if you count the pilothouse with its L-shaped couch and the foredeck *prendisole*. The flying bridge occupies half the housetop, and its furnishings include a second *prendisole*, a large bench seat at the helm, and a six-place padded seat with a table under the arch of the radar mast. With two crew to manage the vessel and serve the *hors d'oeuvres*, and with stunning women in remarkably small bathing costumes among the ship's company, the mood aboard Riva's 66 is always *allegro*.

On the previous two pages are bright, posh spaces in the deckhouse of the Montecarlo 66. Forward in the deckhouse is the pilothouse shown here, with excellent electronics display, big windows, and seating for passengers on an L-shaped lounge. Below decks are the guest stateroom shown above left, the owner's head shown at left, another two-berth guest stateroom, large owner's stateroom aft, and crew quarters for two forward.

LOA: 66'
Beam: 18'
Draft: 6' 1"
Displacement: 80,000 pounds
Power: Twin J&T-prepared G.M. 12V-71TI diesels rated for 726 hp each
Fuel: 6000 liters
Water: 2000 liters
Builder: Cantieri Riva, Sarnico, Italy
U.S. Agent: Riva Yachts of Florida, 612 W. Las Olas Blvd., Fort Lauderdale, FL 33312

Above, just your average spinnaker reach at the Pan Am Clipper Cup. This Dan Nerney photograph of *Tomahawk* summarizes the range of emotions well by focusing on one face: that of the man trimming the spinnaker. Written there is the exhilaration of speed, seemingly unbreakable concentration on the sail's luff, a sense that one false move and we may be broaching, buying a new sail, or swimming, and naked fear.

IMAGES OF THE PAN AM CLIPPER CUP

BY MICHAEL LEVITT / PHOTOGRAPHS BY DAN NERNEY

You know the one about imitation and flattery. Well, the Pan Am Clipper Cup, modeled after England's very prestigious Admiral's Cup, isn't imitating anything anymore. The five-race series, sailed in and around the physically blessed Hawaiian archipelago—which Mark Twain termed "the loveliest fleet of islands anchored in any ocean"—has joined the Admiral's Cup, the Sardinia Cup (a comer in its own right) and the more parochial Southern Cross Cup and the Onion Patch Series in the pantheon of team ocean racing. All the Clipper Cup lacked was a team from Europe—in particular one from the ever-keen English or Germans—to give it true international legitimacy.

What it didn't lack, however, were teams from Australia—three to be exact—and two teams each from Japan and New Zealand, along with three teams from the USA. Another thing it didn't want for was wind—the Trade Winds, overly stimulated by two hurricanes anchored in the area, never fell below 20 knots and typically gusted to 30 and even into the great beyond, until the final Around the State Race. Nevertheless, it blew enough in the finale for *Kialoa* to set a new course record of three days, 23 hours and 49 minutes for the 778-mile course.

The Clipper Cup series didn't lack for drama, either. Ask Jim Kilroy, who in the course of the 150-mile Molokai Race—new this year—broke the boom on his 82′ *Kialoa*, exploded three spinnakers, and dipped the tip of his near-100′ spar into the "peaceable" Pacific when *Kialoa* broached at 22 knots. That particular cleansing instantly wiped $75,000 worth of electronics from the masthead. Ask the boys on *Windward Passage*—that very born-again maxi—which was dismasted in the Around the State Race when the living was relatively easy: 20 knots of winds and seas a diminutive eight feet. Ask "Gentleman" Jim Hardy, the oft-America's-Cup skipper from Australia, a man known to the British crown as "Sir James," about the absent spar on his well-traveled *Police Car*. "What a pity," commented Sir James, one of the world's more civilized knights. Losing similar battles with gravity were the masts on *Dictator*,

Scarlett O'Hara, Gold Coast Express, Zingara, and *Tusbakuro*—and all of this while the crews worried about sunburn. If carnage is the measure of a competition (and for brevity's sake we've omitted a rather lengthy discussion of hull failures), the Clipper Cup may indeed be *numero uno.*

You didn't have to be smart to win here, as you do in Britain's idiosyncratic Solent, where the Admiral's Cup tidalwars are waged. You merely had to be fast and tough, as the theme of this particular adventure in paradise was hook in and hold on. And when the curtain fell on this extraordinary fortnight of ocean racing, the toughest *haoles*—Hawaiian for outsider or Caucasian—were the Americans. The USA Blue Team of *Bull Frog, Great Fun,* and *Kialoa* out-pointed the (Dunhill) Australians, who won the team prize the two previous times the series has run. (There were those who felt that the mesomorphic *Kialoa,* led by that archetypal *haole* Jim Kilroy, should be counted as two boats, but that opinion didn't prevail.) Of special note was the individual victory of *Tobiume,* a Japanese designed, built and crewed boat. This is the first time a boat from Japan has won a major international offshore event.

Haoles have been racing around the state of Hawaii since 1972. The scenery was inspiring, the 778-mile race was particularly challenging, and the natives and not-so-natives were both friendly and physically awesome. But getting to the island of Oahu—2550 miles from Los Angeles, 2360 from San Francisco, and 2675 from Seattle—was not half the fun. The race, sponsored by the small but enthusiastic Waikiki Yacht Club, was in decline because of a lack of participation from the mainland when the yacht club asked an Australian member, Dick Gooch, to try to enlist a major corporate sponsor to fund a series of ocean races. Gooch found Pan Am, which funded and named the Clipper Cup and has made a laudable contribution to ocean racing, not to mention to the color pages of any number of national magazines.

What one remembers most of the Pan Am Clipper Cup is the images of boats buried by their own bow waves, boats on the edge of control, boats belly-up well over the edge of control, the extraordinary Pacific with its crystalline water roiling under the persistent Trade Winds, and the idyllic background of breaking surf and lush high-mountain terrain. This was one of the few sailing events we've covered where the photographers were more excited than the competitors. The racers had that ready-to-be-fed-to-the-lions look, while the photographers strutted around as if they had money in the bank. It was a feast for the lens and the eyes.

Nautical Quarterly sent Dan Nerney to Hawaii to bring back the images on these pages. Nerney, a former Coast Guard officer and Rhode Island School of Design graduate, has written the book on how people see racing boats. Speaking of this assignment, Nerney said, "These were not the windiest days I've ever shot in. Certainly the Admiral's Cup in '79—a couple of those days were the windiest I've ever worked in—but to consistently have five days of wind in excess of 20 to 25 knots all day long is extraordinary." We are pleased to present here Dan Nerney's vivid portfolio of ocean racing in paradise.

Whether *Condor*, above, is the fastest of the maxis is debatable; what is less debatable is the fact that she's the best-looking of the breed. Thus forgive us for lingering on her a little longer in these pages. This Ron-Holland-designed maxi, owned by Bermudian Bob Bell and raced in this series by sailmaker Dick Deaver, finished third overall and second in class to *Kialoa*, also a Holland boat. Holland drew seven boats in the series.

Left, 17 or so color-coordinated crew-members of *Condor* are about to disprove the notion that maxis are dry. Above *Windward Passage* is followed by *Vengeance,* the old *Siska. Passage,* as long in the tooth as they come, having been launched in 1968 to an innovative design of Alan Gurney and recently modified by Doug Peterson, might have owned the maxi class had she not been dismasted in the final State Race.

The Australians, who have won this contest the two previous times, found the sledding tougher this time. Antipodal yachts on this spread include *Margaret Rintoul III,* above left, *Seaulater,* left, and colorful *Police Car,* above. *Margaret Rintoul,* a Frers 51, was second in class; *Seaulater,* an Ed Dubois designed 39 footer, was fourth. Jim Hardy's *Police Car* dropped her pink spar over the side. "What a pity," commented Sir James.

Above, Alan Bond's *Apollo* is chased by *Gerontius*. In his other life, Bond is the prime mover of nearly a decade of America's Cup challengers from Down Under. Right, Class B yachts fight for room and a breath of fresh air. From left to right are the yachts *Zamazaan*, a Farr 52, *Sunbird V*, an S&S design, and *Jumpin' Jack Flash*, which is a product of that talented Kiwi Laurie Davidson, who penned nine yachts in the series.

Above, *Condor* sails to weather of archrival *Kialoa*. Both Holland designs, *Condor* is heavier, shorter, and carries more sail. Right, is *Sunbird V.* The success of the Japanese here, in particular of *Tobiume*, signals the emergence of Japan.

Above, the yacht *Pachena.* Inside her are the Japanese yacht *Super Witch,* sailed by the very occidental Lowell North, and *Police Car.* Left is *High Noon* and an all-wahine crew. The hourglass was typical of her wind-crossed series.

You might say that my sailing career began in the spring of 1911 when I crawled under the door of a shed at the Nevins Yard in City Island. I had gone with my father and a couple of his friends from Bayside, Long Island, to the now-abandoned Bartow station of the New Haven, thence by monorail and trolley to the boatyard. We were there to look over a fleet of ten 30′ gaff-rigged sloops—the Bird Class—designed by the famous William Gardner for our Bayside Yacht Club. Centerboard-and-keel boats, they had an ample cockpit with seats and a little cuddy cabin forward. ☐ Being a Sunday, there was no one around, and we hunted for a way to get into the big two-story building shed. We could see the boats through the windows, but could find nothing open. Finally my father spotted a door on the northeast corner of the building that had an open space at the bottom maybe six inches deep. I was four years old then, just the right size to slip under and try to open the door from the inside—which I did—and we got in to look over the new Birds—one of which was my father's boat-to-be called *Loon*. ☐ My father raced *Loon*, sail #3, with some success, winning at least one club championship, and taking home a number of "loving-cup" prizes, one of which was a ship's clock that now graces the mantel in my daughter Corliss Engle's home in Brookline, Mass. That clock, with its innards now replaced by an electric motor, and no bells working, was won during Atlantic Yacht Club Race Week in 1914 at SeaGate. On Labor Day of that year, *Loon* went down by the stern in a blustery Nor'Wester off Fort Schuyler, never to be found, and I remember standing at the head of the dock at the yacht club when word reached shore that *Loon* had sunk but all hands were saved.

NAUTICAL QUARTERLY

72 YEARS
OF YACHT RACING

BY ARTHUR KNAPP, JR.

Topsiders hadn't been invented in 1922 when the Larchmont Yacht Club's three Sears Cup contenders sat for their portrait. They are, left to right, George Hinman, Arthur Knapp, Jr., and the late Sterling Kryder. Knapp, 15 and looking serious, was skipper. They won the Sears Cup that year, which was the second season for a trophy that was then, and still is, emblematic of the Junior Sailing Championship of the United States.

Living so close to the Bayside Yacht club (three blocks away), as soon as I was old enough I spent all my summers as close to the club and the water as I was allowed. There were rules, of course, about "unaccompanied children" but we never paid any attention to them, and as long as we behaved ourselves nobody said much. The head boatman was a big, wonderful Swede by the name of Cap'n Lawson. Charles G. Lawson was there for many years, beloved by everyone, and his wife, of French extraction, was the chef at the club. Lawson ruled the place with an iron hand—and he had an iron hand, believe me. On one occasion, when my father expected to be away for a long while, he took me to Lawson (everyone called him "Lawson"—even I did at 11 years of age) and he told him that if he had any trouble with me he had parental permission to belt me. Lawson's hands were so big and tough that I took one look at 'em and he never had any trouble with me. Lawson swore like a trooper, and I learned to swear like him at ten, although my parents never heard a curse word from me until I hit my thumb with a hammer one day when I was 17.

I suppose I was taken for an occasional sail on *Loon* up through 1914—I have vague recollections of that—and I must have picked up some knowledge of how to steer a boat, because in 1916 my father gave me a 12′ sneakbox-type Butterfly Class boat that we named *Flutterby*. The price was 20 bucks—think of that! It had a solid, stubby mast—no rigging—and the peak of the gaff-type mainsail was held up by a long, pointed sprit. At Bayside then, there was a fleet of some fifteen or twenty Butterfly Class boats, and we sailed and raced them in Little Neck Bay to our hearts' content. It was a safe harbor for kids—you could stand in very gooey mud at low tide in most parts of that bay, and maybe even dig up a soft-shell clam with your toes. The muddy bottom was full of "piss" clams—at low tide you could stamp your foot and the clams would squirt up—so you dug down with a stick or your fingers, pulled out a clam or two, washed 'em in the clean salt water and gobbled 'em down. No threat of hepatitis in those days.

My father insisted on having manila lines run along the edge of *Flutterby*'s deck to give me something to hold onto if I capsized. I don't recall ever upsetting *Flutterby*—those boats were so beamy and flat for

> The Bayside Yacht Club was a going concern in those days, with a regatta every Saturday for the Bayside Bird Class, the Star Class, the Bayside Bees and the Butterfly Class—no racing on the Sabbath.

their length it would have been difficult for even a kid to dump them. I wish I could say the same for fifty years of frostbite winter sailing. I must have dumped in dinghies 15 times or more over the years.

My grandfather William T. Carleton, English opera tenor and later movie actor—he played opposite Pearl White in a hair-raising serial, "Pearl of the Army," among other features—took the mainsail off my little boat, rigged up some lines to the boom and sprit and then added 15 or 20 Japanese lanterns, lit up that night with candles, for the B.Y.C.'s "Illuminated Pageant" in July, 1916. I was towed around the anchorage after dark by one of the participating yachts, sitting there at the tiller in a sailor hat and suit. It must have been quite a sight, and I was awarded First Prize—a handsome Tiffany cut-glass vase which I still have. It was a "First Prize" in many ways.

The Bayside Yacht Club was a going concern in those days, with a regatta every Saturday for the Bayside Bird Class, the Star Class (some 20 of them), the Bayside Bees and the Butterfly Class—no racing on the Sabbath. The courses, for the most part, were inside the bay, once or twice around various permanent marks. Apparently *Flutterby* did well, for I have still in my files—after all these years—a neatly printed and handwritten card from the American Red Cross acknowledging with thanks receipt of the value of prizes that we won during that summer of World War I.

In the March, 1917, issue of Rudder Magazine, there was a series of pictures—along with little captions of doggerel—called "The Seven Ages Of The Yachtsman, With Apologies To The Bard of Avon." The very first photo—which had to have been taken the summer of 1916—showed a little Butterfly catboat, sail #7, with a small boy (me) dressed in a sailor suit and hat, and another small boy, Bramwell Davis, sailing in front of the Bayside Yacht Club. The pictures go on to show larger boats, motor and sail, a large three-masted schooner (probably *Atlantic*), and then a shot of Biscayne Bay Yacht Club's lower porch (which is still there, rocking chairs and all).

It is my firm opinion that this series of photos—which I have kept and treasured all these years—plus the winning of the Sears Cup in 1922—more of which later on—had a dramatic and tremendous influence on my sailing career. I haven't retired to the rocking chair yet, at the Biscayne Bay Yacht Club or anywhere, and it seems to me that The Climax to that career, which started 70-odd years ago in Bayside, may well have occurred on the weekend of September 11 and 12, 1982, at Newport.

Yacht Racing/Cruising, a very fine yachting magazine, last year conducted a poll to nominate the world's 20 outstanding sailors. Unfortunately, the name of Knapp didn't collect enough votes to make that list, although it has been rumored that I was #21. In any event, when the magazine—later on joined by Timberland Boat Shoes as a sponsor—invited me early last winter to participate in a "Hall of Fame Regatta," I jumped at the opportunity—especially since it was to be sailed in Etchells Class yachts—a really "hot," worldwide class designed by my old and good friend Skip Etchells. Immediate thoughts turned to crew—who should I ask to sail with me? The first was easy, Peter Quigley, 6'4", who crewed with me in the International One Design *Sir Joseph*, Bert Brady's yacht "on loan" for the entire 1979 season. Peter won Larchmont Race Week in 1981 in the Etchells, and he'd crewed with me, my grandson Phillip Engle, and Wilma Bell when we "wiped up" the IOD fleet on Western Long Island Sound. Peter was an absolutely fantastic help in the Hall of Fame series—absolutely fantastic.

I did actually consider two of the real experts in the Etchells Class out on the Sound, but I figured that those guys had been skippers for so long that they'd probably forgotten how to be good crew. I shan't mention their names here, so as not to embarrass them, but they are aware that I had them in mind. Peter Quigley became the "middle man"—I don't know what the hell that means, but I've seen it in many articles about Etchells, and I guess it means the guy who takes the brunt of the crew work. Young Bizzy Monte-Sano had given me a fight talk on Labor Day. He's another hot number in the Etchells fleet and knows what he's talking about. "Mr. Knapp," he said, "Let Peter Quigley set up the boat for you, trim sheet, and you just sit there and steer!!" Since I've always had my hand on every sheet in almost every boat I've sailed, it was a bit difficult, but I never touched a sheet and gave the work to Peter and Roland Schulz. Except for one mark-rounding when the main just *had* to be hauled in (both Peter and Roland were busy doing something else), I hauled the mainsheet until Peter was able to grab it away from me halfway in and we made a very neat rounding. My other original choice for the third member of the crew was not able to handle the dates, so Roland Schulz joined us. Roland has grown up around the Larchmont Yacht Club and raced for years in the Rhodes-19s with his father and brother. Recently, he has been crew for Joachim (Joe) Schulz-Heik in Joe's Etchells, and they have done very well indeed during the past two years. Roland is a very fine foredeck man and really handles the spinnaker very well—and very quickly.

So there we were with two expert Etchells crews and an overage, arthritic, large (I won't say fat) almost one-eyed skipper—suffering from an injured Achilles tendon for the past two months to the point that I wasn't sure it would allow me to compete. We got there early—to be prepared and ready for the practice race on Friday. We got ourselves organized and went out for that practice race—taking seventh out of ten starters—definitely not a good beginning. I do not throw it out as an alibi, but the bottom of our boat was full of blisters—it wouldn't point and it

THE
RUDDER
MARCH 1917.

Seven Ages of the Yachtsman

BY
SAMUEL A. WOOD

WITH APOLOGIES TO
THE BARD OF AVON.

At first the handy catboat takes his fancy,
And as he sails he sees a vision fine
Of greater ships, built by the necromancy
Of glowing boyish dreams, speed through the brine.

wouldn't foot. The 15 new suits of sails provided by the Cressy Loft of Horizon Marine Enterprises were lovely sails, and could not be faulted. However, in that particular boat we couldn't and didn't go well. The first day we ended up in tenth place, but the second boat we drew—provided for the Hall of Fame series by Bob Sides—performed very well for us when we steered it the right way.

In a discussion with my crew, we elected to try and stay clear of any crowded ends of the lines or any messes. I decided early on that we'd try and get what I call a "Louis Piana"—i.e., we'd start on the right end of the line—at the Committee boat—and tack immediately onto the port tack. I have—in starting my Shields ten minutes after the Etchells got started in YRA events on Long Island Sound—watched Louis take this end of the line almost always. He doesn't seem to care whether he is on the gun, or a few seconds late. Immediately he tacks onto port and takes off. Sometimes it works for him, sometimes it doesn't but he almost always does it. For us it worked very well. And in the race on Sunday, the fourth race of a five-race series, we got a beautiful start. In fact, as I recall it, all our starts were good. We tacked over and were off and running, the boat pointing and footing like a scared cat. It wasn't long before we were in an obvious first place and we stayed there for three mark roundings—with loud cheers and screams from the assembled gallery—much louder than for anyone else, we all thought. I didn't realize I had so many good friends out there. Unfortunately, on the fourth leg—downwind—Jobson and Melges jibed on either side of us before we did, and when we did go over I managed to steer into a dead spot. We were in third and remained there—again to screams and yells and horns at the finish.

In the fifth and last race—this time with some good tacks and jibes engineered by Peter Quigley—we managed another third place, giving us fifth in the Hall of Fame Regatta. The screams, cheers and horns sounded again and, believe me, it "warmed the cockles of me heart." I stood up and waved furiously to everyone—not a victory, no, but not a bad finish for a 75-year-old mental, dental and physical cripple. Earlier on, I said something about a "climax" to my long sailing career. Many times I have been asked which victory did I think was the best, the most thrilling? Was it being in the afterguard of the great J-Boat *Ranger,* successfully defending the America's Cup in four straight races? Was it winning the Star Worlds in 1930? Was it winning five YRA Championships in several International One Designs? Was it taking second in class in *Dorade* in the Bermuda Race of 1930? Was it ranking at the top in 14 out of the first 19 seasons at Larchmont in the Interclub Frostbite Championships? Was it skippering the 74' yawl *Baccara* to second place—just about her only prize—in the 1976 SORC's Nassau Cup Race?

I can't really answer that question, but I do think that taking fifth place in this fall's Hall of Fame series was pretty doggone close to the top,

Our dreams are realized by easy stages --
The boy gives up the centreboarding sport,
And, for a season, zealously engages
In powerboating of a modest sort.

But that is much too tame for his ambition,
And he invests in meteoric yacht
Or power ships that scurry like perdition
For cups and glory -- and the lord knows what!

perhaps even The Climax. Sure, Gary Jobson won a clear victory, and Bud Melges was not far behind, nor was Dave Ullman far behind him, and it is no blot on my escutcheon to have "The Great Dane," Paul Elvström, finish only a point and three quarters ahead of me. Gary Jobson, Buddy Melges and Dave Ullman deserve many kudos for taking first, second and third; but I am still screaming from the rooftops about Knapp finishing fifth in that league—the one and only Hall Of Fame Regatta. Ya' know, it ain't doing so badly to knock off the likes of Hobie Alter, Bob Bavier, John Bertrand, Steve Benjamin, Dennis (himself) Connor, Bruce Kirby, Lowell North, George O'Day, Eric Tabarly, and Dr. Stuart Walker—even if it was only a five-race series.

Readers will forgive me, I hope, for tooting my own horn. And I hope they will come with me now to hear some softer notes from 65—!—years ago. It was in 1918 that my father traveled to Buenos Aires, selling woolens for J.P. Stevens. Sometime in the late summer, I wrote him a short note: "Dear Father: There is a Star Boat for sale at Bayside with two suits of Ratsey sails for $250. I would like it. Love—Arthur." P.S.— Father bought it for me. This boat, *Southern Cross*, had been owned by Herbert F.L. Funke—and while, yes, it carried sail #62, it was actually #3, built by Ike Smith in Port Washington in 1911. A previous owner of those two boats had, for reasons of his own, changed the numbers, a practice that became illegal later on. Like all the other Stars of the time, it was gaff-rigged, and it stayed gaff-rigged until 1920-21 when the Star Class changed over to the marconi rig. It was in 1929 that the class adopted the present taller rig and sail plan. For a couple of years after the marconi rig was adopted in 1920—with little or no money available—I used my gaff sails on the new mast. They seemed to work OK—at least I made em work.

Southern Cross started a love affair for me with Star Boats that lasted through 1932, and then picked up again in 1946 when I won the Arms Trophy at Noroton, Conn., with Wilma Bell as crew, and she won the ("Shucks") White Trophy in Pat O'Gorman's *Wahini*. A Star Boat was a "small" boat in 1918—no such things as Lightings or Blue Jays or Comets or Sabots. Nor were there any junior sailing classes or instructions. That didn't come for another six or seven years. Pequot Yacht Club started a junior sailing course about 1923, and it was 1929 before Larchmont developed classes. At Bayside we were on our own. There were several other boys like myself who had Stars at 12, 13, 14, and 15, racing in the local fleet of some 22 boats, and occasionally sailing around to Manhasset Bay to take part in their activities.

For a few years, we were so young that our boats had to be hauled out for the winter at some local boatyard, but pretty soon all of us took care of our own Stars. We each owned "four-poster" cradles—put out at low tide and weighted down with stones or old iron. Our boats were floated in at

The racing sloop with canvas vast distended
 Has lured him from his fleeting love of steam
Or gasolene, whichever he expended
 To take him through the third stage of his dream.

His interest in racing craft he's losing
 The ardor of his youth is on the wane --
A handsome schooner yacht invites to cruising
 In placid waters of the Spanish Main.

high tide, then we waited for low water and rolled them up above the high-water line with block, tackle, planks and rollers.

I raced *Southern Cross* regularly until 1924, the year I entered Princeton, and sold it for $400 to help pay for my education. To encourage me, Father offered me a quarter for each boat I beat. Pickings were slim for a long time, but one day in Larchmont Race Week I managed to place third in a fleet of 28 Stars. That cost him $6.25, no small sum in those days. My father said "That's all, brother, you are on your own!"

One Friday afternoon before Larchmont Race Week in 1919, my father sailed with me across the Sound to Larchmont for me to enter Race Week. We asked at the club for the race circulars, which they gave me as a participant, but wouldn't give Father unless he was planning to race or was a member of the club. Since he was not going to race, he told them that he'd join the club. This led to his becoming a member of the Race Committee, under the aegis of Howell W. Perrin, and later to my becoming a junior member at age 13. And that, in 1922, led to my becoming the winning skipper of the Larchmont Junior Crew for the Sears Cup, along with George Hinman and the late Sterling Kryder. It also led to my taking second place in the Tub Race on Ladies' Day in July, 1922. (Ladies were not at that time admitted to the club on any day except Ladies' Day in Race Week.) That was Water Sports Day—swimming races in front of the club between the main float and the "Flub-Dub," a large barge with a bathing house on it, along with tub races and canoe tilting. The tub was wood, about 3' across, and you sat in it and paddled furiously with your hands. If you paddled too hard you sank.

That membership also led to my crewing, along with my father, in the very first Bayside-to-Block-Island Auxiliary Race in 1921. This was a race started that year by the BYC for auxiliaries in which they allowed you to take on and use exactly 25 gallons of gas anytime you wanted—to and around Block Island and back to Bayside. We were aboard the 35' yawl *Sakana,* owned by J. Henry Esser of Larchmont. I'm happy to report that we won this first auxiliary race in 33 hours against *Sagola,* owned by Bert Hinman of Larchmont, who had among his crew his son George Hinman. This auxiliary race blossomed and boomed, and I went on it for many years. *Sakana* had a cement keel, the lead having been removed for the war effort. The heavy seas off Block Island loosened up the keel bolts so that *Sakana* leaked like a basket. The pumps clogged, and I recall spending a lot of time passing up buckets of water from the bilge to my father to keep her afloat.

In 1922 William Ulysses (Boston Bill) Swan, dean of yachting reporters in Boston, came down to Larchmont to persuade Commodore James B. Ford to send an entry to the newly organized (1921) Sears Cup Races for the Junior Championship (under eighteen years of age) of the United States. Dick Thayer of Eastern had won it in 1921.

And now in ship palatial he is floating --
He has the joy he pictured would be his
When, as a boy, he loved to go catboating --
Ah! here is boundless luxury -- and fizz.

This is his goal. In gentle retrospection
The Admiral of Veranda Fleet of Rest
Finds of all captains in his recollection
The little catboat skipper pleases best.

Boston Bill convinced Commodore Ford that Larchmont should send a crew, so George Hinman, Sterling Kryder and I (skipper) were sent by train to Marblehead for the series. It was sailed in Alden "O" boats—a little 18-footer that is still being raced in various places. We lived upstairs in the Eastern Yacht Club, and the last I heard those rooms were still there.

I am quite sure that Commodore Ford paid all the expenses of our Larchmont crew that was sent to Marblehead for the Sears Cup Races—he generally paid the deficits of the club during his tenure as Commodore of Larchmont from 1915 to 1928, and made many other contributions. I am happy to report that his faith in us was not misplaced. We did win Commodore Herbert Sears' Paul Revere bowl, although I will be the first to admit that we were very lucky indeed.

Commodore Ford owned the Victory Class sloop *Blue Jacket*, a Gardner designed class that came out just after WWI. The late Drake H. Sparkman sailed this boat for the Commodore for a number of years and won a number of championships on the Sound. The Commodore also owned and raced one of the Larchmont "O" class sloops, another Gardner design and much larger than the Marblehead "O"s, being about 50' long. He put one of the very first marconi rigs in this lovely sloop and, believe me, he cleaned up with it in this class of about five yachts. Some of the Larchmont "greats" who sailed on the "O" boats were Harry Maxwell, Jack Johnson, Gerry Ford and his brother "Cappy" Ford, as well as the ebullient Butts Whiting.

Cappy Ford was a plumber in New Rochelle, but he raced with the best. The story is told that one evening, ashore at Fishers Island, where he'd been crewing with Harry Maxwell, they were all at a very fancy, sort of "arty" dinner party. The hostess asked Cappy just what he painted. "Well, nothing but the ends of lead pipes—I'm a plumber," said Cappy. "Please, Mr. Ford, have some more of this and more of that," said his hostess. "This is the first time I've ever had a plumber in my house that it hasn't cost me a lot of money."

Butler Whiting, one of the "O"-boat Greats, was the authority for the maxim that when the typical Long Island Sound Sou'Wester was West of Sou'West, you should take the port tack first if you were going up towards Execution Rocks and if it was South of Sou'West you went off on the starboard and crossed as quickly as possible to the Long Island shore. It *always* worked. But now—30-40 years later—that Sou'Wester has, in my opinion, been well loused up by all the buildings and ribbons of highway on Long Island—no trees to speak of, no grass, just all buildings and concrete. The typical Sou'Wester of yesteryear came off the ocean, a somewhat cool or chilly breeze. And now it blows through all the heat reflected off the buildings and the cars on the roads and bounces up over the Sound to land somewhere in Connecticut. It has also changed its direction somewhat, so you can't go by Butts Whiting's theorem very

At the start of a Star World Championship race off Execution Rocks in Long Island Sound in 1931. Arthur Knapp sails *Peggywee* (#455) on a fast beat with her owner Newell Weed as crew. They finished a disappointing 13th in the series. They had won the Star Worlds at Gibson Island in the Chesapeake in 1930, a series that featured a "hair-raising" final race.

often. I know I'll get an argument on this, but I'm correct as hell, 'cause I'm out there racing and I've seen it happen. What's worse, I've been "skunked" by it often in the last 15-20 years, so there is no doubt in my mind at all.

As the winning Sears Cup skipper I was presented with a little sterling silver medallion or logo of the Eastern Yacht Club, about the size of a silver dollar. I used it as a watch fob for years in school, sneaking a surreptitious peek at it every once in a while in class, and I kept it until John Shadden of Long Beach Yacht Club in California won the Sears Cup in 1980. Then an idea popped into my big head.

John's father, Tom Shadden, was Commodore of Long Beach Yacht Club in 1980, so I approached him with my idea. It met with his approval, so I went ahead and designed a trophy by inserting my ancient Sears Cup medal in a thin piece of Lucite™ together with an appropriate inscription plate held together by two thicker pieces of Lucite™ bolted together and set on a varnished block of Honduras that had been in my possession for more than 40 years—a sort of combination of modern and traditional. The dedication to the Long Beach Yacht Club on the little plate inside said that this trophy was presented to LBYC in honor of John Shadden for winning the Sears Cup 58 years after I had won it, to be "presented for whatever purpose the Flag Officers of the Long Beach Yacht Club felt proper." They flew me out to Long Beach for their Annual Dinner in 1980, where the award was presented with great éclat and where it was given to John Shadden himself for the first year. Last year (1981) Barney Flam was the worthy recipient.

While this is somewhat out of chronological order, perhaps I should explain my connection with Long Beach Yacht Club and the Shaddens. In 1964 Donald Leedom—a registered "rep" for E.F. Hutton in Long Beach—came to New York and told the senior partner that he'd like to "meet Arthur Knapp and go to the New York Yacht Club." The senior partner checked with a partner in the firm of Carlisle Jacquelin, for whom I was a commission broker and member of the Stock Exchange. In those days, when a partner of a "customer" firm asked a favor, believe me, the odd-lot partners (and commission brokers—me) jumped! I took Don Leedom to lunch at the Stock Exchange Luncheon Club, got him on the floor of the Exchange as a guest, and then took him to dinner at the New York Yacht Club and showed him around.

The net result of that little fun deal was that I was invited to the first running of the Congressional Cup match-race series at Long Beach in 1965, to be sailed in Cal-40s. I was invited not only that year, but also in 1966 and 1967. With a Larchmont crew in those years, we finished fourth, fifth and sixth—in that order in time. In 1968, with Don Leedom as Commodore of the club, I was made their #1 Honorary Life Member and presented with a sterling-silver membership card. And I have been invited every year since to take part in the Congressional Cup in March as a judge. I've missed only twice in those 17 years.

> We beat Clinton Crane boat-for-boat—no flukes—and he was a real hotshot sailor of those days—by having my crew of three kids hang over the rail "Starboat" fashion.

In 1974, with my ego blown up by a victory in the National Championships of the Shields Class in 1973, I managed to get myself invited again to sail in the Congressional Cup. With a very fine crew, but a bum skipper, we managed to finish tenth—and brother, that's last. In 1981, the Long Beach Yacht Club honored me "over and beyond the call of duty," a really wonderful and heart-warming honor, by dedicating the whole Congressional Cup week to me, their #1 Hon. Life Member. What a great and exciting week that was.

That was recent history for me—now back to my ancient history. It was in 1923 that I came closest to getting involved in a "shotgun wedding." I had taken a nice blonde classmate of mine, one "Pilly" Palmer, out to Execution Rocks, the starting line for a Star Boat race. When we finished there was no wind, and no tows came along (as they frequently did), so I ended up paddling my *Southern Cross* eight miles home. It was 9:30 at night by the time we drifted up to the dock at Douglaston where Pilly lived—tired, hungry and otherwise distressed. The only thing I wanted was to get her off the boat so I could obey the call of nature. Her father, a Midwesterner who knew from nothing about boats and winds, met us at the dock madder than a wet hen—the only thing he lacked was the shotgun. "Daddy" Palmer had telephoned my father earlier, who thought it a huge joke and laughed at him, telling him to relax and that we'd paddle in eventually.

I was selected by our Bayside fleet of Star owners to crew for John R. (Jack) Robinson in his *Little Bear,* #61, in the Star World Championships in the late summer of 1924 off Execution Lighthouse on Long Island Sound. We won that Star Worlds, and that fall I entered Princeton—with a scholarship fortunately. I waited on tables at Commons, delivered newspapers early every morning, had a job as usher at football games, and in my senior year became head usher and received a nice fat check—fat, that is, for those years. With some financial help from two very generous uncles, Edgar A. Knapp and Ralph P. Buell, and good marks (to hold onto that scholarship), I managed to get through Princeton financially as well as have time to try out for freshman football. After a couple of weeks they just ignored me, so I dropped football and went out for crew.

Elected to the Princeton Terrace Club with a so-called "managership" which gave me a free room in my senior year, I kept on with my rowing, and in my senior year gained a seat, #3, in the 150-pound crew under the coaching of Gordon Sikes, Prin. '16. This was the crew captained by Jimmie Thompson '28, and we won the Goldthwaite Cup from Yale and Harvard as well as beat Columbia and a couple of other 150-pound squads. However, I must admit we missed our chance for the Henleys in England when we were defeated in Philadelphia by the Penn 150s. For winning the other races we were given our Minor Sport Championship "P" letters. If you could see me now at 208 pounds, you'd wonder how I was ever on the 150-pound crew. Believe me, it wasn't easy—I had to "dry out" before every regatta for several days.

The years 1924 through 1928 were a turning point in my young life—crewing in 1924 in *Little Bear* for my first international yacht racing victory, being on my own at college—all the various things that happened to me during those four years influenced my "growing up" and ended with a job as a clerk on the floor of the New York Stock Exchange that fall of 1928 at fifteen bucks a week for the "odd lot" firm of Jacquelin & DeCoppet. Somehow or other, during the next 46 years on the floor of the Exchange, I managed to get time to do a lot of racing, onshore and offshore, summer and winter. As I look back on it, I wonder how I managed to get time off to do it all.

During those Princeton years there was work to be done in the summers—no loafing around. In the summer of 1925 I spent my time selling WearEver kitchen pots, using an old Ford Model T coupe as a conveyance. I don't recall that I made much money, but I sure demonstrated to a lot of my mother's friends—who let me use their kitchens—how to bake a potato or even a cake on the top of the stove.

In 1926, I took a summer job as tutor with the family of the late Frank Willock in Dark Harbor, Me., teaching Ruth Willock, aged 15, Latin every morning. She had to read two books of Caesar during the summer. After breakfast I'd sneak upstairs and check out what we'd have to read that morning in a "trot" that I owned. Ruth thought I was very smart. After that I'd take her younger brother Roger out in his Crowninshield-12 for a sailing lesson. My father wouldn't let me take this position until he had consulted with Herb Stone, editor of Yachting—afraid of professionalism. Herb said, "Let little Arthur do it...It'll help him in college and it's a fine thing for the growth of yachting." It is still true that one can teach sailing without taint of professionalism.

On weekends, the two kids and I would sail with the Gallatin girls in their Crowninshield-17. My recollection is that we won a lot of races, but that the highlight of the season was a rescheduled long-distance race of some 25 miles around Isleboro, with a long beat over to Camden, then up the coast some distance, and then through the back passage to Dark Harbor. We beat Clinton Crane boat-for-boat—no flukes—and he was a real hotshot sailor of those days—by having my crew of three kids hang over the rail "Starboat" fashion. Clinton Crane never forgot that race. Whenever we met for years after that he would congratulate me on having shown him how to race his boat right.

In 1927, I took another summer job with another Princetonian family, John T. Arms, Prin. '10, the famous etcher. He had two boys, John Taylor, Jr., 10, and Henry Noyes Arms, 8, and we sailed one of those ubiquitous

> That first regatta was held in the middle of June in three
> lovely Anker 8-meters... Only two races were necessary, for we Princetonians won
> both of them, while Yale and Harvard split.

18' "0" boats. I also sailed with John Arms, Sr. and Henry Rennell in the "S" boat *Ruth,* in which we won the season championship. With the two boys and the former Lucie Bedford as crew we also won Larchmont Race Week in a very large "S"-Class fleet. I still have—and use—the very heavy silver vegetable dish donated for that week by "Capt. E.P. Alker" (the engraving says). That was another good summer, for I had many friends from my junior racing days in Southport.

I graduated from Princeton in early June, 1928, and the next event very shortly was the first intercollegiate regatta ever held. It was at Southport, Pequot Yacht Club, between Yale, Princeton and Harvard. The Princeton University Yacht Club had been founded the previous fall, mostly through the efforts of Charles E. Hewitt of Locust Valley, a classmate and the first PUYC Commodore. I was one of the dozen or so founding members and still am (I think) the Honorary Commodore.

That first regatta was held in the middle of June in three lovely Anker 8-meters owned by Jack Schiott, Robert Gair and Wilder Gutterson. How they could trust us college guys with their gorgeous new boats—only a few weeks in the water—I'll never know. They did limit us to working jibs and mains, but no spinnakers. Briggs Cunningham and Oliver May of Yale had stirred up and promoted the regatta, and George O. May, Oliver's father, had presented a trophy that had to be won three times for permanent possession. John Valentine was the Yale skipper, along with Briggs and Oliver May and others as crew. The Harvard Skipper was John King. My crew consisted of Charles Hewitt (our Commodore), Rufus (Bud) Smith, Robert Garland, Henry Bodman and the late Charlie Bookwalter.

Only two races were necessary, for we Princetonians won both of them, while Yale and Harvard split. The following year, that great sailor, C. Sherman Hoyt, took a hand and the Intercollegiate Regatta was held at Oyster Bay in "S" Boats with Yale winning. In 1930 and 1931, Princeton won each year and the retired May Trophy was put in the gym at Princeton, where it later burned up in a fire that destroyed the building.

However, in 1930 Bill McMillan, Prin. '28, had donated the McMillan Trophy, which is still being raced for at Annapolis in Luders yawls. In 1930, under the leadership of James Pease, Prin. '31, the Intercollegiate Yacht Racing Association was formed and has become a countrywide organization. May I add that the formation of the Frostbite Yacht Club on Jan. 1, 1932, spread the small-boat gospel later on to the intercollegiate group and has resulted in college dinghy racing throughout the country. As one of the founders of both intercollegiate racing and frostbiting, I am very proud to have been a small part of the growth of both.

I became part of the crew of Bill McMillan's 52' Alden Schooner *Merry Widow* in the Bermuda Race of 1928. I am happy to report that we took second in Class B and had a fine sail to Bermuda. The final dinner was held at the New Windsor Hotel, and I recall a turtle about a foot and a half across that had the run of the lobby. I also recall drinking too much of the best Scotch available, Highland Nectar, and being so sick that I can't stand the smell of the stuff to this day.

That year during Larchmont Race Week I steered the famous 6-meter *Lea* to victory. The trophy is in the Larchmont Yacht Club. Next was a trip to Gravesend Bay and SeaGate Yacht Club with Briggs Cunningham in *Colleen,* the fast and famous Star belonging to F.T. Bedford. We won a Lipton Cup for Stars—primarily because we were smart and took advantage of a very strong outgoing tide. We were towed down there by *Parthenia,* a 110' diesel yacht, under charter to Briggs' mother. Later in August, having been selected by the Central Long Island Star Fleet at Southport to crew for Joseph F. Watkins in the Star World Championships at Newport Harbor, California, Joe and I took off for the West Coast, while the boat, *Okla,* #455, was dead-headed out there by the Luckenbach Steamship Lines.

The bottom shelved so quickly off the beach to 3500' or more that they had great difficulty in setting marks. We discovered too late in the first race that you had to sail into about the third roller off the beach before tacking offshore. There was a current down the shore, same direction as the wind paralleling the beach, and you just *had* to go in as far as possible. The first race we went offshore, got skunked and finished something like 12th out of 20-odd. We were smarter after that and wound up second in the Worlds to Prentice Edrington of New Orleans.

Prentice was promoting another Lipton Series in New Orleans later on and invited me to take part, with the loan of Joe Watkins' *Okla.* The boat was again dead-headed to New Orleans and I went through the Panama Canal on the same Luckenbach freighter—as a passenger. In the last race of that series, with a comfortable lead, I fouled Edrington and got thrown out. I seem to recall that I just missed taking home another trophy. Lipton Trophies for the Stars were almost a dime-a-dozen in those days, for Briggs won another one with *Colleen* on the Chesapeake that same summer.

Joe Watkins' Star #455, *Okla,* was swapped to Newell Weed in

Corny Shields developed the International One Design Class in 1935-36, and Arthur Knapp sailed several of the first 25 that were delivered to Long Island Sound in 1937. Shown here is *Bumble Bee*, the boat that William H. Stanley bought in 1944 for Arthur to race with the owner and his daughter Wilma as crew. They raced *Bumble Bee* for ten years, winning three YRA Championships and never finishing worse than third. They also won several IOD Season Championships and led the IOD fleets in four Larchmont Race Weeks and several Manhasset Bay Race Weeks, among other triumphs.

> We caught and passed him and, at the same time, put a couple of boats between us. This was a real "garrison finish," and it gave us the Star World's Championship.

I think it appropriate to point out that all the work I did on the bottoms of various boats paid off, just as did being sure that every other detail, piece of gear, line or block, was just right and in proper working order," writes Arthur Knapp. Here he works on the bottom of *Bumble Bee*. Below, Arthur and Wilma Bell pack a spinnaker "just right," Arthur flaking the sail and Wilma Bell liberally sprinkling the turtle with Johnson's Baby Powder, a trick that lets the sail out more smoothly in a spinnaker set. They raced their boat right.

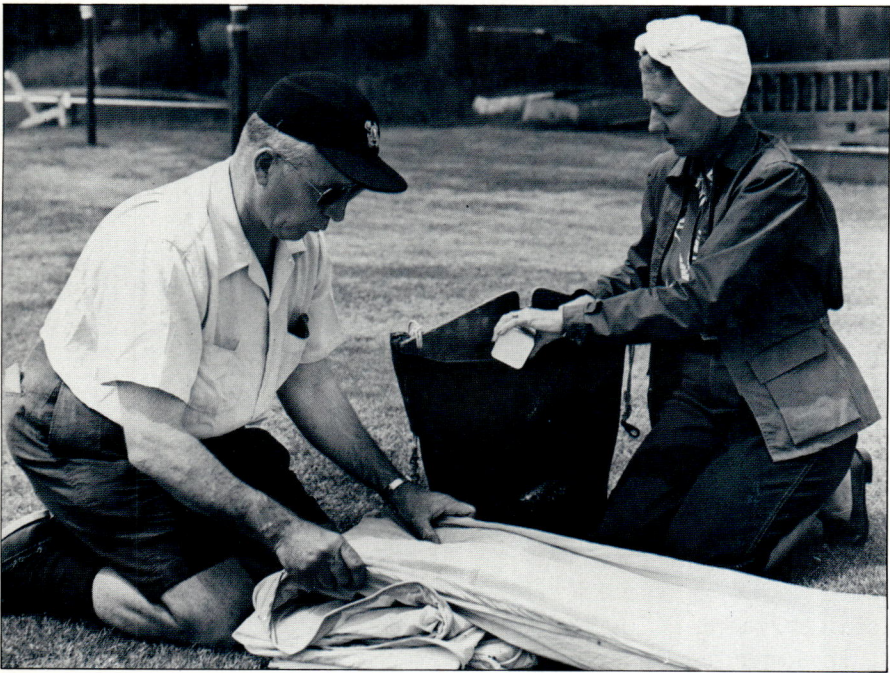

exchange for Newell's fast boat built by Parkman, and renamed *Peggywee* after Newell's daughter Peggy. A deal was arranged the next summer for me to sail her with Newell as crew. We were off and running with a friendship that lasted many years. We raced several Stars, a 6-meter, a Long Island Sound Interclub (*Chinook*) and a Seawanhaka Schooner (more commonly called a "pushwater") named *Scimitar*. And finally my red-headed daughter Corliss, who was born shortly after Newell's wife died of pneumonia, was named after Corliss Weed.

Newell and I won the 1929 Star Eliminations and were in New Orleans at the Southern Yacht Club when the 1929 stock market crash started. We finished fourth in that series with *Peggywee*, and Newell started to lose his shirt. But in 1930 he was still in business in Wall Street and we again won the Western Long Island Sound Eliminations and trucked *Peggywee* to Gibson Island in the Chesapeake aboard a ton-and-a-half Ford flatbed truck. We won the Star Worlds there in a hair-raising race, the last contest of the series.

At that time, Stars were using a three-times-around course—or they could use it—and the last day of this series they did. It was blowing pretty hard, and most of the boats elected to reef—as we did and as Walton Hubbard did. Walton Hubbard, from Newport Beach, Calif., had won the Star Worlds on Narragansett Bay in 1927, and was leading us on this last day of the series by a point or so. I don't recall the first windward leg too well, but I do remember that Walton was leading us by a couple of boats at the weather mark. With nothing to lose at that point, we shook out our reef and did much better on the second beat—gaining a lot on Walton but still not ahead of him. On the leeward leg this time he shook out his reef. On the final beat, we caught and passed him and, at the same time, put a couple of boats between us. This was a real "garrison finish," and it gave us the World's Championship. It is interesting to note that this was the last year that the old low rig—marconi, of course—was used in the Star Worlds. It didn't go as well in light air as the newer and taller rig; but in a good, hard breeze the old rig was a bit faster when properly sailed.

I joined Olin and Rod Stephens—and their father, Rod, Sr.—in *Dorade* for the 1930 Bermuda Race. With a crew of very young men—almost all under 21—we managed to get a second in Class B, beaten only by Commodore R.W. Ferris in his *Malay*, a 45' Alden schooner, who also won the Bermuda Trophy that year. It is interesting to note that 24 years later another *Malay*, sailed by Dan Strohmeier, son-in-law of Commodore Ferris, won the Bermuda Race hands down in a Concordia-39 yawl.

Dorade had been built at the Minneford Yacht Yard in 1929, and I just "happened in" one afternoon and caught Rod, Jr., working hard deep inside her. She was a narrow boat by 1929 standards, and there were old fogeys who opined that she'd never get to Bermuda with that tall Marconi

> In 1936, after Mel sold *Kenboy*, I raced *Ariel* with Charlie Stuart of Halsey Stuart & Co., and we ended up second, about five ten-thousandths of a percentage point behind Corny Shields.

rig—"no rig to go to Bermuda in—should be a gaff-rigged yawl!" But *Dorade* made it, and she did well—always. I admired her and praised her to the skies to Rod, and next thing ya' know I was invited as crew. That started a most happy friendship that has lasted all these years—53 of them to be exact. I've raced with the Stephens boys and I've raced against 'em—and I have praised their abilities to the skies to anyone who'd listen (and many have). They are, in my humble opinion, the outstanding designers in this whole wide world. And why? Because they complement each other—Olie is the designer par excellence, and Rod is the practical expert who lays out the deck fittings and gear. One is the theoretical guy and the other the practical one. It's pretty tough to beat that combination.

I don't really remember much about that 1930 Bermuda Race—nor the subsequent races in 1932 and 1934 when I was aboard *Dorade* again. But I do know that we worked hard and kept the boat going, and that it was mostly on the starboard tack—with the fabled "Bermuda High" taking over. There was one deal that I managed to put into operation on *Dorade* in some of the light airs we encountered in the Gulf Stream. On my Star we often pulled the foot of the main in and the luff down by means of a piece of reef line tied from the gooseneck to the first slide on boom or mast. This had the effect of making the mainsail fuller and baggier for light air.

Just the other day I was talking with Rod about the famous "Cunningham" or "Cunningham hole" that is in general use on almost every mainsail in the whole sailing world. The story that I've always been told is that Briggs Cunningham late one Friday afternoon—after closing time at Ratsey's loft—gave them a sail that was too long on the luff, a cotton mainsail from one of his 6-meters. He wanted it shortened, but it was too late to do anything. George Colin Ratsey is said to have put in a grommet about six inches or so up the luff rope, along with instructions to use a piece of reef line to snug down the sail to the gooseneck fitting and thereby make it possible to tighten the luff above the grommet. That grommet—more thoroughly reinforced, of course—has spread around the world and has become known as a "Cunningham." Rod Stephens suggested to me on the phone a few days ago that this thought had developed from our system on *Dorade* of pulling down the first slide in the luff, or pulling in the first slide on the foot. Whether this is the real background, I'm not prepared to say—nor to argue the point—but I pass it on for what it's worth.

Rod and Olin have never been receptive to booze in any form, but they had no objection when their father, Marshall Rawl and I wanted to put on a cocktail party one evening in Hamilton Harbor—way out in the middle where all the other racing boats were then anchored. That party lasted all night—honest injun—and with daylight we were all swimming about the harbor, Olin and Rod as well.

The years 1931 and 1932 were definitely not successful ones for Newell Weed and Arthur Knapp in Stars. We won the Eliminations in '31, but finished in 15th place after being thrown out of a race for barging. In 1932, racing Larry Reybine's *Lout,* we were thrown out for being over the line before the start and therefore lost the Eliminations. However, we did a little better that year in the Long Island Sound Interclub Class yacht *Chinook,* finishing third in the Season Championship.

Chinook was loaned to us by George Lauder at the suggestion of Corny Shields. Corny was a great one for getting new people into the Sound Interclubs to improve the caliber of the racing. Throughout the next 20 years he was always pushing to get new talent into whatever class he was interested in at the time—Sound Interclubs, International One Designs, and later the Shields Class, a lovely boat he had Sparkman & Stephens design, and then promoted all over the country by giving fleets of boats to colleges with the financial help of his brother Paul. Corny gave seven Shields boats to SUNY Maritime College, and then arranged for them to be chartered to yachtsmen around the Sound during the summer when the cadets were on their cruise. I myself have skippered Shields #197, the *Wm. E. Tuthill,* for ten years on this "semi-charter" deal, and have done quite well with it—four YRA Championships and one Shields National Championship in 1973.

Corny arranged for me to sail *Kenboy* in 1933, Sound Interclub #7, which belonged to Melville O. Griffiths of Larchmont. Mel, his brother Fred, my first wife, the former Dorothy Roan, and I raced *Kenboy* to victory for three straight seasons—1933, '34 and '35. We had exactly one suit of sails, by Ratsey & Lapthorn—no problem there as to which suit of sails we'd use under various wind conditions. But we cleaned up the class—so "max nix." In 1936, after Mel sold *Kenboy,* I raced *Ariel* with Charlie Stuart of Halsey Stuart & Co., and we ended up second, about five ten-thousandths of a percentage point behind Corny Shields. That was a close one, less than one boat between us. Had we beaten Corny on the finish line, *Ariel* would have been the champ.

During 1935 and 1936, Corny Shields had been very busy organizing a new one-design class. He had fallen in love with the 6-meter *Saga,* owned by Eldon Trimingham of Bermuda. Designed and built in Norway by Bjarne Aas, she was a beautiful "Six" to behold. Corny got Bjarne Aas to do a slightly smaller boat, which he called the International One Design, and 25 were delivered in the spring of 1937 to the Sound, while other smaller batches eventually went to Bermuda, Marblehead and Northeast Harbor. I might add that the class is popular in England, Norway and Scotland still, and that a fleet was recently "discovered" even on the south coast of France.

Per Lorentzen, of the prominent Lorentzen family of Norway, had an

Arthur Knapp sailed Bermuda Races with the Stephens brothers and their father aboard *Dorade* in the 1930s, and aboard *Mustang* with Rod Stephens, Jr. in the 1950s. Here is the *Mustang* crew in Bermuda in 1956: from left, Arthur Knapp, Robert Erskine, Jr., Clayton Ewing, Dr. Gifford Pinchot, Rod Stephens, Mrs. Pinchot and Stuart T. Hotchkiss.

IOD there when the family had to flee the German invasion. His boat was taken over by a German officer, who cared for it and raced it. Per got it back at the end of the war and brought it to our fleet at Larchmont. It has been said that the "jig" for the IODs was hidden by the Norwegians and brought out after the war to build more of them. In the 1980s, the class is prospering again, with the two fleets in Marblehead and Northeast Harbor building new boats of fiberglass. There are now three molds around the world, and the boats are abuilding all over the place, the remarkable thing being that the wooden boats and the fiberglass boats weigh within a couple of hundred pounds of each other.

I was invited by my sister Allegra and her husband at the time, James B. Brickell, to race their IOD #13, *Allegra,* in the very first series in 1937 for a trophy put up by the Race Committee Chairman, James D. Sparkman. I am pleased to report that we won that series. The boat is still around under the ownership of Joe Weed, one of the prime movers over the years in the class. Altogether, I raced seven or eight different Internationals, some for only a race or two, others for a whole season, from 1937 until 1953. Then I took them up again in 1979 when Bert Brady loaned me his *Sir Joseph,* IOD #7, which we raced most successfully—winning all but one series that summer with a crew composed of my 15-year-old grandson Philip Engle, Peter Quigley (who was the main reason we did so well in the Hall of Fame Regatta this past fall) and, of course, that superior crew of 40 years in the IODs, Wilma Bell.

Starting out our first full season in the International Class in George Esselborn's *Myth* in 1941, then in 1943 in Bill Luders's *Four Winds,* and finally for ten years in *Bumble Bee*—which William H. Stanley bought for me to care for and race—we took five firsts, six seconds and one third—nor should I forget a number of Larchmont Race Weeks and Manhasset

> John Nichols always put *Bumble Bee* at the bottom
> of the yard, for he said I used so much water in working on the bottom with
> wet-or-dry sandpaper that I'd flood the place.

Bay Race Weeks. Only Bus Mosbacher has won more YRA Championships, and those over a longer period of years.

I said above that Pop Stanley bought *Bumble Bee* for me to race. He had sailed a few races with us in 1943 with his daughter, Wilma Bell, also in the crew. It was, of course, during the war. Pop had retired from the food brokerage business a few years before that and had sold his interest in the company. With only an "A" card for gasoline for their Cadillac, Pop and Mom Stanley weren't able to drive very far to go out for dinner—as was their custom. Pop told Clint Bell and myself to get him some figures on the cost of running an IOD. The result was his purchase of #14, which was renamed *Bumble Bee* (sometimes known as "the floating salmon can") because, as Pop told us, he'd made the money to buy the boat selling Bumble Bee salmon and tuna. Although he'd never raced before, Pop caught on very quickly and handled the jib halyard, lift and foreguy with aplomb and efficiency. He was a very fine crew, a most cooperative owner, and fun to sail alongside of. We had a delightful and successful ten years.

The arrangement Pop and I made was that I would take care of *Bumble Bee*—do the sailing, painting, varnish work and whatever else was necessary. Pop would pay the bills. The only change from that was that John Nichols—at whose yard in Mamaroneck we kept the boat—wouldn't let me do the topsides. He said I wouldn't know how to do it properly, so he and his brother Sonny took on the job and did it perfectly—no streaks and no overlaps. John always put *Bumble Bee* at the bottom of the yard, for he said I used so much water in working on the bottom with wet-or-dry sandpaper that I'd flood out the place.

I'd work my heart out on the bottom, sanding, filling, touching up, then sanding, filling, touching up again—all with a lot of freshwater hosing in between. Work on the bottom was one of the more important things in my book. It just had to be smooth and slick, and I spent many long (and wet) hours to get it just so.

I will say now that there were times when Knapp wasn't that smart, and it amazes me how long it took for me to figure some things out. With *Bumble Bee* it was my practice to have her hauled out the week before Larchmont Race Week to make doggone sure that her bottom was right. I'd set my alarm for 5 AM, go up to Nichols Yacht Yard and work with a hose and wet paper until 7 or 7:30, go home, shower, shave, eat breakfast, then go into Manhattan to the Stock Exchange. The close was at 3 PM. I'd dash for the 3:25 train to Larchmont, change and get up to the yard again, and stay until maybe 6:30 or 7. Next morning, the same deal all over again, until the boat went overboard on Friday. On a number of occasions, when we'd have light air, it would amaze (and anger) me that some other boat that hadn't been hauled would sneak by us. How could this happen?

The light finally dawned in 1958 when the first postwar America's Cup series was held. Word came to me via a fellow Odd Lotter, John Reid, who had a cousin working on *Sceptre* in Scotland, that they planned to have some tubes, little ones, in the bottom below the stem which would exude a detergent. The idea was to make the water "wetter" and make the boat faster. Not having a boat of my own at that time, I gave this word to Olin Stephens. He tested it in the tank—by putting detergent on a hull model—and found that it seemed to make the boat 1 to 1½% faster on the wind. That would be good—roughly—for something like 20 lengths on the eight-mile beat that was in vogue then.

I sponged some Lux or Ivory Liquid on the bottom of my frostbite dinghy, *Agony*, that winter. She went overboard in a shower of suds, believe it or not, and seemed to go better in light air. I then recalled that during the many winters I had raced dinghies I would sometimes get a very smooth paint job on *Agony* just, just before the season started. Some other years, being too busy or too lazy, I'd just throw the boat in the water. The realization came to me that when I really had the bottom freshly painted and smoothed up it didn't go; when I just put it overboard it went very well. Aha, said I—the new paint was tacky and sticky and the water wouldn't flow by as easily; but when the bottom was untouched, unpainted and unrubbed, the old and "cured" surface was hard and fast.

It is interesting to note that the idea of tubes to supply any such liquid has now been banned by the Rules. After becoming skipper of *Weatherly* in 1958, I often thought of applying a detergent while she was on the ways, but it is quite obvious that any such stuff would be long gone by the time she traveled the ten miles to the America's Cup Buoy.

In passing, I think it appropriate to point out that all the work I did on the bottoms of various boats paid off, just as did being sure that every other detail, piece of gear, line or block, was just right and in proper working order. That's the sort of preparation that pays off in races won—everything in order and working perfectly.

Thoughts on the early years of the International Class bring to mind that in the beginning there were no hard and fast rules on sails. Starts in those days were—in the prevailing Sou'Westers—to leeward. And there were lots of Sou'Westers. Some starts were off the black can at Execution Rocks—others were off the Larchmont mooring buoy. Frequently the first mark was gas buoy 42 off Scotch Caps or a special black-and-white nun off Parsonage. This meant a run or a very broad reach, and then a beat across the Sound to Weeks Point, or "Corny's Corner." Corny's Corner was a red gas buoy way up in the mouth of Hempstead harbor. Corny just loved that mark, and he was always pushing the Race Committees to use it. It was, believe me, a good choice, because it made for a gorgeous long windward leg.

The only problem with it was that the first boat to round the leeward

> It is very interesting to note that, as the years
> went by, the same guys won—and then there was a cry and holler to go back to being
> able to use sails from whatever sailmaker you wanted.

We two are the *only* charter members of the Frostbite Yacht Club from Jan. 2, 1932, who are still even semi-active in frostbiting," writes Arthur Knapp on the back of this photograph. Holding the polar-bear symbol of the illustrious F.Y.C. are Arthur, in N.Y.Y.C. cap and heavy sweater emblazoned with the name of his frostbite dinghy, and Howard Kraus, Chairman Emeritus of the F.Y.C. They started something in 1932, and the winter dinghy-racing season is now observed by scores of yacht clubs in the U.S.

mark took off like a shot and headed for Long Island, never to be caught. In a true Sou'Wester (as I have pointed out earlier in comments about Butts Whiting, Sr.), you should get to Long Island, but fast, and it worked every time.

With no tight sail rules in effect then—and done perfectly legally—Frank Campbell bought a Ratsey main with one helluva big roach to it for his IOD #2, *Rascal,* adding a fair amount of area to the sail. He'd take off on the first reach or run and get to the leeward mark some 15 lengths ahead—never to be caught. This, of course, brought howls of indignation from many others in the class and led to all one-design sails, drawn by lot from a hat. It is very interesting to note that, as the years went by, the same guys won—and then there was a cry and holler to go back to being able to use sails from whatever sailmaker you wanted. I might point out that this identical situation came up from time to time in most other one-design classes—obviously with the same general results.

One more vignette of the wonderful International One Design before I get to the Frostbite Yacht Club and 50 years of dinghy racing. About 1952,

Wilma Bell and I had been crewing aboard that fast S&S yawl *Good News* on the New York Yacht Club cruise. We finished the cruise at Gloucester and, by pre-arrangement with a great friend—and a super sailor—Simmie LeBlanc, we went to Marblehead to go racing with Simmie on an International he sailed as crew. We went aboard this IOD and met the owner, an old gent now long gone. As we sailed about Marblehead harbor on a boat which, believe it or not, still had the original double-jibstay, double-jib tack fittings, and double halyards that had come from Norway in 1938 (kinda behind the times wasn't it?), the owner suddenly said, "Ya' know, we don't race with ladies on this boat." "You don't?" I questioned. "Well, in that case just take us over to that nearest dock and we'll get off." Which we did. Imagine a jerque like that; Wilma Bell is the fastest and most able crew I have ever sailed with—man or woman, small boat or large. When a genoa on a big 60-footer needed trimming, I've seen Wilma reach for a winch handle while some big guy was just getting off his fanny to tail on the sheet.

The upshot of that stuffiness was that we borrowed IOD #1, *Ariel,* by telephone to Tom Boynton in Boston, scrubbed the bottom off Eastern Yacht Club with one of their pool guys, who also crewed with us, and beat all of the Marblehead IOD experts, including the two Hood brothers. That nasty ole guy finished a bad last! Poetic justice of a sort, I have always thought. That race stands out in my memory for two reasons—the above tale, plus the fact that we won it by using our masthead fly to the "nth" degree. The air was extremely light on the last leg, but there was a new Southerly coming in that showed on the fly at the top of the mast but didn't fill in down low. It was an unusual situation, making the lower part of the mainsail look as though it were luffing badly—so everybody trimmed in flat. Noting the beam wind indicated on the fly, we made the most of the top of our main and gradually drifted past the boats near us to cross the finish line in first place. A satisfying victory—don't forget that the Hood brothers were there, too.

Editor's Note: Arthur Knapp's memories of 72 years of yacht racing—from his trip into a Nevins building shed at the age of four to his latest exploits at the age of (now) 76—will continue in Nautical Quarterly 22. Author of that sailing classic, *Race Your Boat Right,* winner of more silverware than any other round-the-buoys sailor alive, and participant in much of what has been significant in American yacht-racing history over six decades, Arthur has more lively stories to tell. In the next issue, he'll tell about 50 years of Frostbite dinghy racing, campaigning the great J Boat *Ranger* in the 1937 America's Cup series, skippering *Weatherly* in the Cup trials of 1958, Shields Class competition on Long Island Sound, and much more.

A few of the Knapp collection of trophies are shown here. They represent nearly 70 years of silverware collecting, and the few items here are, Arthur guesses, "about 3%." The first of Arthur's trophies was first prize in the Bayside "Illuminated Pageant" in 1916. Others were for the BYC's Season Championship in Butterfly catboats, the 1922 Sears Cup, first (with his father) in the 1922 Bayside-Block Island Race, winning crew in the 1924 Star Worlds, winning crew in the S-Class Season Championships at Pequot Yacht Club, 1924 S-Class honors in Larchmont Race Week, winning 6-Meter skipper in 1928's Larchmont Race Week, first (with Newell Weed) in the 1930 Star Worlds, three first places in 1933, '34 and '35 in Sound Interclubs in the YRA of Long Island Sound, winner of the first series of IOD races in 1937, skipper of *Nyala* for second-place among five 12-Meters in the 1938 YRA Championship Series, 1942's YRA Championship in IODs and 1943's IOD Season Championship, three other YRA Championships in IODs between 1944 and 1953, IOD victories in 1979 in the YRA Championship, Season Championship, Larchmont Race Week and Manhasset Bay Race Week, winning skipper in Frostbite dinghies for 14 of 19 years (1946-1977) in the YRA of Long Island Sound, Shields Class National Championship in 1973....

DAISY

BY STAN GRAYSON

The first time I saw *Daisy*, she was drifting on Lake Winnipesaukee. I stood in the slippery grass next to the water and squinted but couldn't see anybody aboard. Then the morning silence was broken by a muted sort of puttputtputt, and Jim Doughty's head and shoulders popped into view as he took his place at the steering wheel mounted on the port side of the cockpit coaming. He was there for about a minute, heading towards the dock, when the motor stopped and he disappeared to crank it up again. It took rather a long time that morning to get *Daisy* from her mooring to shore.

Daisy is a 22′ torpedo-stern launch built by the Lozier Motor Company in Plattsburgh, New York, in 1905. At that time, the company turned out such boats, and larger ones, by the hundreds, each equipped with a two-cycle or four-cycle engine of Lozier's own design and manufacture. The smaller boats got the two-cycles, the larger models—some were 50′ or more—had four-strokes.

At the beginning of the century, there were many such companies competing in an active launch market and publishing catalogs that boasted the virtues of their work—the wood, the design, the craftsmanship, the safety, the durability. Now all those companies are gone and so are most of the boats. It is difficult to say how many launches survive or have been restored. *Daisy* lives on a mooring, like a waterborne dowager, surrounded by younger Chris-Craft runabouts. Lozier launches are certainly rare items. Jim Doughty knows of perhaps a half-dozen. Other Lozier buffs claim to know of others, tucked away here and there in barns and

When she's running, Jim Doughty's *Daisy* is a graceful, beautiful way to travel on a lake's glassy surface. When she's being fussy, the gloves go on and the tools probe the real mysteries of her 1905 gas engine.

boathouses, but nobody believes the grand total could number much more than twelve. Few have, as does *Daisy*, a Lozier one-lunger nestled between the engine bearers. *Daisy*, it is clear, is a rarity.

Jim Doughty has done his best to keep the old launch as authentic as possible. His unwillingness to alter her engine is one reason he had such difficulty that morning, but occasional malfunction is something Jim Doughty is willing to suffer. He insists on keeping *Daisy* as close as he can to looking and acting just as she did when she was launched from Lozier's wooden boat shed, on the shores of Lake Champlain, nearly 80 years ago.

The road into Jim Doughty's New Hampshire weekend place is narrow and winds among pine trees. There is one particularly tight turn, and when you round it you see a red, white, and blue sign nailed to a tree—Interstate 95. Doughty's cottage stands a few hundred yards further down the dirt road. It is surrounded by trees, and under several of them old motorboats lie in cradles covered with tarpaulins. There are two workshops. In one of them rests a Lozier launch that predates *Daisy*. It is a fantail model to which somebody has added a cabin. Doughty plans to restore the boat, just as he did *Daisy*.

Before *Daisy*, he owned a 1955 Chris-Craft runabout which he restored himself and kept in the Wolfeboro yard run by George Johnson. That place is a kind of Chris-Craft heaven and a clearinghouse for many antique and classic boats as they come on the market. It was George Johnson who put Jim Doughty in touch with *Daisy's* owner when the old Lozier was about to be sold by the family that had owned it for many years on Lake Champlain. "We took a weekend trip to see the boat," Doughty remembers. "We had high hopes and a couple of Polaroid pictures the owner had sent us. We bought the boat."

The Lozier's graceful hull had been sheathed in fiberglass. The original engine had been replaced by a Model A Ford conversion. Jim Doughty took out the engine and began removing the fiberglass. "It came off okay," he says, "but the resin remained. What chemicals couldn't get off, I had to sand and scrape." He replaced part of the keel and half the ribs. The rotted portion of keel surprised him because, when he had inspected the boat, he had been unable to poke his knifepoint into the hard wood. When he got home, he found he had been prodding cement. When he got that out, he found the rot. The decks were entirely replaced. The cypress hull planks, however, were in good condition. He routed the seams and recaulked. "I worked on her for three years of long nights and long weekends."

One of the few survivors of the hundreds of launches built by Lozier, *Daisy* had the good fortune to fall into the skilled hands of Jim Doughty, who "worked on her for three years of long nights and long weekends."

Although he sold his Chris-Craft, Jim Doughty remained in close touch with George Johnson. It was Johnson who told him about a 3-hp Lozier engine. It had belonged to an engine collector in upstate New York, and when he died the collection went up for sale. Doughty bought the Lozier engine, sight unseen, for $500. It didn't even need a paint job. "I never dreamed," he says, "that I'd ever find a Lozier. The only two I knew of were up on the St. Lawrence and they were in the museum at Clayton. Later I found out about another one in the Finger Lakes region and about some parts. If you need a part, all you can usually do is pray or have one made." He has only a few spares, among them an igniter.

Although he now owned both a Lozier launch and a Lozier engine, Jim Doughty found he was short of information on how the two should be joined. He culled methodically through all the Lozier literature he could obtain, noting details of the engine and how the company suggested it be installed. Because the pages of one catalog were stuck together, he did not know about the hot air drum that sends exhaust-heated air from the muffler to the vaporizer. Later, when the engine proved balky and unwilling to run while cold, he began asking questions. But there was nobody he could find who could be of any real help. He went through his catalogs again and again.

Because of problems he associated with the engine's vaporizer, Doughty considered replacing it with a Schebler carburetor. He refrained from doing so out of determination to keep the engine original. Besides, the vaporizer was mounted on threads unlike the standard threads required by the carburetor. It was as if Lozier had devised its own threads just to make things more difficult. Finally one day he unstuck the pages of his catalog and learned how the vaporizer was supposed to be warmed by hot air from the muffler. By then, the launch had already been fitted with an underwater exhaust, not a muffler, so Doughty "freelanced" a preheater arrangement. He also located a prop shaft with a reversing propeller in Brookfield, New Hampshire. The shaft fit the boat perfectly, says Doughty, but looking under the floorboards at the machinery, one gets the impression that the installation must have been more complicated than that.

Daisy does not have one of the original Lozier fuel tanks, although her owner says he knows where one is and thinks he may try to buy it. The company offered several tanks. The standard version was a cylindrical model, but those who wished to have additional capacity could order a tank shaped specifically to the bow section of their launch. On *Daisy*, the fuel

line no longer runs outside the hull. Her owner is less worried about the results of a fuel leak than he is about additional holes in the boat's bottom.

As his restoration project neared completion, the only thing Doughty despaired of finding was one of the handsome bronze builder's plaques that Lozier had mounted on each of its boats. The only plate he knew of belonged to a family of Lozier enthusiasts in Plattsburgh. They loaned him the plate, and a jeweler and old-boat hobbyist named Syd Marston made an exact replica for *Daisy*. "He wouldn't take a nickel for his work," says Doughty. "That's how things often work in the hobby. People can't wait to help you out."

Gradually, after much trial and error, *Daisy* began to near wholeness. The original steering cable, made of tinned copper or brass, had stiffened up and was replaced. The brass wheel and the steering winch drum, the latter turned from mahogany, are original. Finally, the old launch was good as new. She was slipped into Lake Winnipesaukee and the sunlight sparkled on her white hull and yellow varnished-oak deck and coamings. She reminded Jim Doughty's wife, Priscilla, of a daisy, and that was how she was named. *Daisy* has been awarded several trophies at the annual antique boat meets held in the summer on the lake.

Living with a technology that will soon be a century out of date has its moments. Jim Doughty has had plenty of chances to ponder this, but he tells himself that having things go wrong is, after all, merely a part of the old-boat game. "The first year I had the engine," he remembers, "I had all sorts of problems. It is very, very temperamental." The old one-lunger soon developed a personality, and its major trait was moodiness. "When it gets in one of its moods," says Doughty, "I don't care what you do. It just won't run. That vaporizer is," he held his hands palm upwards and searched for the words, "something else."

By the time Jim Doughty became the engine's owner, a lot of hands had passed over its gleaming exterior and delved into its mysteries—to little advantage. Doughty found the vaporizer to be the source of a complex of maladies, each more quizzical than the one before. He took the device apart and found that instead of there being merely one spring inside to seat the valve, there were three. Which one was right? Which had the correct tension? He noticed that the valve guide was worn, too. He lapped the valve in its seat with compound and put a new bushing in the guide. He chose the one spring that seemed most "right" and assembled the vaporizer. He did all this and built the preheater, too. It all helped, but it

A replica of the bronze builder's plate that The Lozier Motor Co. attached to the forward coamings of their boats was one of the final touches of Doughty's meticulous and all-but-original restoration project.

did not insure a reliable machine.

No matter what has been done to the engine thusfar, it usually seems to require attention of one sort or another. Sometimes its moodiness finally gets to its owner and he walks away from the boat. In the summer of 1980, when it was over 100 degrees out on Lake Winnipesaukee, the engine stopped and just would not start. Starting it requires a degree of muscle and optimism at any time, and that day all of Doughty's optimism drained away. He paddled *Daisy* home in disgust. Later, when he returned to examine the engine, he found the trouble to be two loose screws in the timer. "I was out there all that time and I never noticed those two screws." Because the igniter hammers away incessantly, every nut and bolt in its linkage must be perfectly tight. The result of a loose nut is a balky engine.

The day Jim Doughty and I went out in *Daisy*, the engine was feeling moody. The boat looked beautiful, its brass polished, its varnish gleaming, but the engine seemed to resent having someone aboard who had come to poke and prod and photograph it. It was a warm morning in July but not warm enough, apparently, for the vaporizer's liking. By the time *Daisy* finally reached the dock, Doughty was shaking his head. "I think this is one of its moody days," he said. His daughter had gathered an optimistic-looking pile of equipment on the dock, just as if things were going to work out, and there was no reason to think the engine wouldn't cooperate.

"This used to be a clean T-shirt," said Doughty, looking at an abstract of grease stains. He knelt before the engine, reached for the flywheel starting handle and heaved it upwards. The Lozier came to life immediately. With its underwater exhaust it ran with relative quiet, a sound like many pieces of steel whispering to each other. For a few moments, *Daisy* strained hopefully at her dock lines. Then the engine slowed and abruptly died. "Maybe it just needs to get warmed up a bit more," I suggested, hoping the words would make us all feel better.

"Maybe that's what it is," said Doughty. He took the gear as I passed it down from the dock, stacking it on the plush red naugahyde seat cushions. During the next 15 or 20 minutes the engine ran many times, but never for very long. Doughty removed the stationary electrode, which on the Lozier is mounted in the center of the cylinder head. He put a screwdriver down the hole until it rested atop the piston. Then he rotated the flywheel, watching to see when the igniter broke contact. The engine was timed perfectly. Almost regretfully, he screwed the electrode back and wiped his hands with a rag.

On the assumption that the engine would like things more if we cast off from the dock, thus displaying our faith, we started the machine again. The Lozier thumped powerfully, and we breathed sighs of relief and settled back to enjoy the ride. The manner in which one of these old launches moves through the water has to be experienced to be appreciated. *Daisy* sliced silently along, leaving little wake and riding smoothly. "With these old displacement hulls," said the owner, "you don't get your brains beat out." We had just begun to really savor the boat when the engine stopped again. "Miserable," said Doughty.

That sort of thing, unfortunately, characterized the whole morning, but we did not give up easily. Once, I happened to be looking right at the vaporizer when the engine died. "Did you see that?" I asked. Jim Doughty shook his head. "That time, when she stopped, a puff of blue smoke came right out of the vaporizer." It was as if the valve was not seating properly. We went back to the dock and took the vaporizer's top off. Things looked normal inside. Doughty performed a few minor adjustments and we tried again. That day the engine never did run for longer than 10 minutes at a time. The owner was most apologetic and obviously unhappy. I got the feeling that he finally was tired of the Lozier's moodiness and that he contemplated something drastic—a new-fangled Schebler carburetor, perhaps.

"Don't do anything drastic," I told him. I had been stranded too many times by old boats and old cars to be much surprised by this one's performance. "I'm going to do something," Doughty said.

It was a couple of weeks before I talked with Jim Doughty again. "How's the boat?" I asked. "Fine," he said. "After you were here, I took that vaporizer off and brought it down to a machine shop. We found out the spring was not seating the valve reliably all the time and made up a bushing to insert in the valve guide." He sounded relieved, as if he and the old Lozier had at last come to terms. The last time we spoke, *Daisy* had just been hauled for the winter. All through the autumn, her 75-year-old engine had run just fine.

Editor's Note: This far-from-rare adventure with a rare old boat is adapted from a chapter on Lozier launches and engines in Stan Grayson's new book, *Old Marine Engines*. The publisher is International Marine, 21 Elm St., Camden, Maine 04843; the price is $22.50; and all 224 pages are delightful, to say nothing of authoritative.

One of the few Lozier boats still powered by a Lozier engine, this one is a rarity. And so are her engine parts. "If you need a part, all you can usually do is pray or have one made," says her owner.

PHILIP C. BOLGER
BOAT DESIGNER, GLOUCESTER, MASSACHUSETTS
BY JOSEPH GRIBBINS

When you call Phil Bolger on the telephone, the voice that answers says "Bolger." It used to ask a pointed "Yes?" It is a curt, Boston-accented voice, and there is an intimation of "What do you want?" in the single word it pronounces, a thing that makes the caller feel that he's interrupted something. He has. What he's interrupted is a thought process that's been going on for 50 years, with many such interruptions but with probably no real disturbance of its flow or its complexity. ☐ Phil Bolger is thinking about boats, an intellectual and technical exercise whose ideal is a purity the designer seems to prize above all things—a rightness, an exquisite equilibrium that extends not only to what he calls "designs that are right of their kind," but to peripheral bits of perfection: the way the lines go down on paper, the way the parts of his recent small boats come neatly out of 4' x 8' sheets of plywood, the way the designer spends his workday, the way he expresses himself in person and in print.

Phil Bolger traces a careful curve on design #434 in his workroom at 250 Washington St., Gloucester. A few of these 400-odd boats have been designed for himself, and the latest is *Resolution*, which ties up to a pier in the Annisquam River just below the Route 128 bridge and takes the ground with aplomb when the tide is out as she is shown doing here. *Resolution* is a 48' x 11' double-ender with a pair of low-aspect lugsails on a ketch rig, a "cheap and powerful" arrangement the designer borrowed from a 19th-century British drift-fishing boat, the Mounts Bay lugger. The spars are counterweighted so that one man can bring them down on deck, and Bolger singlehands this sizeable vessel on daysails and short cruises. He hopes eventually to live aboard, wandering the ICW and doing design work at the desk and drawing board in her big amidships cabin.

Bolger is inspired by thoughts of boats that will be pure and perfect, but unbothered—so he says—by boats that incorporate the "crude solutions" he cheerfully admits in a lot of his own work.

Bolger is precise. He is also funny, self-deprecating, easy to challenge on dogma, free with conversation when he's in the mood for it, and oddly anti-precise in his libertarian tolerance of new and strange ideas. Conversations with Bolger, when he gets rolling, skip sideways from yacht design to politics, ancient history, the space program, sex, money, any number of things. And they are full of quotes and footnotes from H.G. Wells, Alexander the Great, Kipling, Mary Renault, W.C. Fields, any number of people. Although he works in a field that he claims is "really not worth the time of really able people," he gives it his time every workday and, one suspects, pretty much every instant, awake or asleep with dreams of an ultimate portable daysailer or some dead-simple outboard workboat. Bolger is inspired by thoughts of boats that will be pure and perfect, but unbothered—so he says—by boats that incorporate the "crude solutions" he cheerfully admits in a lot of his own work. "Some boats are better than others; but it's not important that they be better," he says in a conversation about the uses to which various types are put.

He means this "any sort of boat will do" in the general sense that a boat roughly suitable to its purpose can achieve its purpose, and in the social sense that it's good for people to enjoy themselves on the water whatever they're in, so long as they don't get drowned. But in a very thoughtful article he wrote for this magazine's ninth issue, Bolger described L. Francis Herreshoff's H-28 as "a deliberate mediocrity" in concept, but a boat that "if built *exactly* as designed down to the last detail (and the details are defined on sheet after sheet of large-scale drawings)...moves from mediocrity to a universal prototype, original essence of small cruising boat...It's a haunting and frustrating achievement. Generations of young designers and boatbuilders have tinkered with it, trying to make it faster, or roomier, or something. The result is always a mediocrity that *looks* mediocre. In context, different means spoiled. There's a lot to be learned from studying this design; but to apply the lessons you have to start over with a blank sheet."

In several remarks in his latest book for International Marine, Bolger illuminates his unique, austere approach to shaping boats. *Burgundy,* his sharpie variation on the L.F.H. *Rozinante,* is able to be built by Brad Story for less than a third of the cost of a *Rozinante* on the shop floor that looks like a Stradivarius. "There's a catch," writes Bolger. "*Rozinante* is one of the all-time masterpieces of art. For visual satisfaction, three *Burgundys* don't equal one *Rozinante*. Notwithstanding Brad's Yankee outrage (at her cost to build), I think the *Rozinante* is worth what she costs. But for somebody who doesn't have the price of a Rubens original, there may be some merit in a Playboy centerfold"—(i.e., Bolger's lovely *Burgundy*).

In discussing *Wisp,* a canoe-form 20′ sloop built by a man who gave her the best of materials and finish, and didn't mind building three trunks for a pair of bilgeboards and an inboard rudder, Bolger notes: "This is a goldplater, something I'm seldom immediately comfortable with...I tend to go off and try to produce something cheap and expendable that will do the same job." And writing about the angled, shield-shaped transom of *Fancy,* a lovely 15′ gaff sloop of Muscongus Bay inspiration, Bolger discusses the uselessness of such a stern and concludes: "I've often thought of offering a reward for a good reason why pretty girls shouldn't chew gum. A legitimate excuse for a stern of this kind would be welcome in the same way, as it makes me uncomfortable to draw something degraded in its action by its aesthetics."

There is a tension here between perfect but elite little boats like Francis Herreshoff's masterpieces and the boats for everybody that Bolger has designed with inspired inventiveness for decades. It is a creative tension for the designer. Bolger has drawn his share of goldplaters, and some of them boats that were exquisitely right, when he or the client gave the work few restrictions of time, money or materials. But yacht design is a game for Bolger, and limitations of time, money and materials are rules in the game. It is a game he enjoys playing, and the goal is to achieve boats that are beautiful, well-behaved, safe in a variety of mischances, and a pleasure to be in. They should also be simple in structure and rig, undemanding in maintenance, and easy on their personnel. These final qualities define Bolger's version of the game. He has applied himself to bringing simplified and frequently cheap boats closer to his own ideals of rightness for nearly 30 years, and more than a few of his 433 designs to date have come close. A very few, in the designer's careful judgment, have been close to perfect. But they are different boats—the title of one of Bolger's four books for International Marine—and they are products of different mental processes from those which produce designed-around-the-rule IOR boats, competent copies of traditional Yankee workboats, or even never-before-seen multihulls and performance powerboats.

Bolger's grandfather was an inventor, which may account for his grandson's inventive fervor in terms of genes. Among other influences, it probably does account for his freedom and freshness of vision. Thomas Patrick Bolger came to Boston from Prince Edward Island, an eager immigrant who "was a plumber who turned into an inventor," according to the designer. Grandfather Bolger invented things to be made out of steel that had previously been made out of wood, and his principal invention—"the one that made money"—was the steel icebox. Others were a very efficient ash sifter for coal furnaces and a plant box that irrigated itself. "He was an ingenious contriver," says his grandson, choosing his words precisely, and he was a man who had a safe full of granted patents when he died. Phil Bolger's father, William A., was salesman and business agent for the family company that sold the steel iceboxes "all over the place," in Latin America and Bermuda as well as in the U.S.

"My mother's people were master fishermen and vessel owners on both sides," says the designer, "but not in my time." The Cunningham family of Cunningham & Thompson of Gloucester owned the celebrated fishing schooners *Arethusa* and *Ingomar*, among scores of others, both built early in this century by Tarr and James in Essex, Massachusetts, from designs by Tom McManus.

William A. Bolger died suddenly in 1934, and it was a crisis for the family, although Phil, then seven years old, doesn't recall hard times. His mother, Ruth Cunningham Bolger—still a vigorous woman at 89 who keeps the house in Gloucester that she helped design with her husband and a perhaps overwhelmed architect, and still plants the flower garden with its hedge of lilacs—coped and carried on through the Depression so that her younger son never noticed much change. "She is a woman of strong character," says Bolger.

Phil's brother Bill, who he describes in contrast to himself as "a competent type," took a hand in his upbringing, being a fatherly ten years older, and gave the future yacht designer his first boat. "My brother thought it would be interesting to build a boat out of Masonite... It didn't work out at all well, so he gave it to me. He had made a skate sail, which I took, and he taught me to make the hardware for the sail and the boat in my grandfather's shop... It didn't sail very well, but I can say that I had a boat with leeboards, an unstayed mast and a wishbone boom 45 years ago."

Phil Bolger's "first real boat"—although the Masonite contraption would seem to be very real in terms of influence—was a 16' Chesapeake catboat designed by Ralph Wiley and built by brother Bill, a legacy to the younger brother when the older went off to war. "It was a very exciting boat to sail—big rig and nose-heavy," Bolger recalls. It was a boat that Bolger sailed until he followed his brother into the Army. Phil Bolger is of that generation that had its adolescence during World War II, and it is the generation that produced the Hell's Angels and now-forgotten bouts of "chicken" on the highways as games of courage to counter elder brethren who had experienced The War. Bolger went to Bowdoin to study History, but he was soon seduced by soldiering. "I called up a friend to see what he was going to do," Bolger remembers of that first summer after a year of college. "He said he was going into the Army, and I made a snap decision to go with him... We were determined to be good soldiers—infantry soldiers—to do it right." Bolger and his friend were warned by the sergeant in charge of the exams that if they didn't score well they would end up in the infantry, so they "tried to figure out the wrong answers."

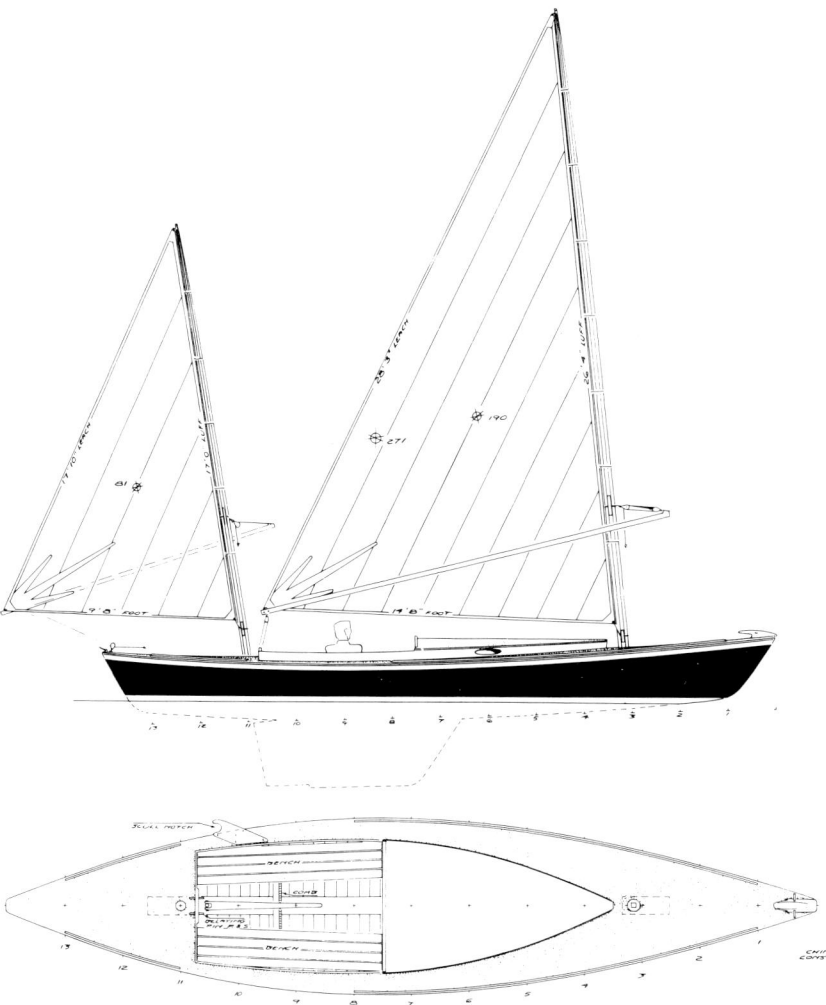

BURGUNDY

"*Burgundy* is built of the same materials as *Rozinante:* oak and pine, bronze and lead. The work would be done with the same care, and she ought to last as well, which is to say, indefinitely. She's the same length, breadth, and draft, and her cockpit and cuddy are comparable. The cuddy doesn't have the deep footwell, but it has more sprawling space. We thought of replacing the *Rozinante's* canvas easy chair with a couple of folding aluminum beach chairs.

"*Burgundy's* action in rough water won't be as smooth, but she'll throw a lot less spray, and she's much more buoyant for her weight so ought to be more forgiving of bad handling and bad luck. In a fresh breeze she's almost certainly the faster of the two."

—from *30-Odd Boats*

> This first published design elicited "a satisfying
> amount of correspondence—probably three letters," and it caused Bolger to
> set up on his own in the house in Gloucester...

They didn't succeed. Bolger went to the combat engineers and his friend went to field artillery. Bolger was in the 1st Cav. in the Army of Occupation in Japan for a year, and he was, in his own judgment, "extraordinarily incompetent," although a crack shot on the rifle range.

"When I got out I went back to college on the G.I. Bill and wasted three more years studying History," he says. He graduated cum laude from Bowdoin, and he took with him not only laurels but a distaste for what he indicts as "an academic establishment that is wrecking American civilization." Bolger describes himself as "a card-carrying Libertarian," and he feels that students who learn on their own, and get good at something, should have the same access to professions as students who have gone through the motions of acquiring an academic ticket. Bolger soon sought a ticket in yacht design, a thing that, true to his principles, seems to be granted on performance rather than school credentials. When Bolger was back at Bowdoin, Lindsay Lord published *The Naval Architecture of Planing Hulls*, and Bolger wrote him a letter that questioned some detail in the book. When he graduated, he was invited up to Falmouth Foreside, Maine, to work as a draftsman. Lindsay Lord was designing "very striking—spectacular—houses then," Bolger remembers. But it was a good apprenticeship in boat design. "Doc is certainly a very brilliant man," says Bolger of this versatile designer whose powerboats were very adventurous in the 1940s and 1950s. "No praise is too great for his generosity to me."

Bolger worked for Lindsay Lord for less than a year before Lord recommended him to John Hacker in Detroit, a fast-boat wizard who was busy with contracts for the U.S. Air Force. "It was, for me, a gathering of confidence," Bolger says of his months with Lindsay Lord, "and that was one of Doc's talents." With Hacker, Bolger needed all the confidence he could get. The company that had contracted the rescue boat for the Air Force—the Huron-Eddy Corp.—was what Bolger describes as "a menagerie of boat designers." The boat was the largest hull that Hacker had ever designed, a 90-footer, and it had three Packard engines with vee drives and with the props under the engines. Hacker had designed raceboats like this, and the project should have been a piece of cake, but the old man seemed to be much too responsible to the Air Force. "Jim Eddy, who was in charge of the weights, would come in and tear his hair over the extra structure that Hacker kept putting into it," Bolger remembers.

Bolger remembers a lot more illustrative things from his months with Lindsay Lord and John Hacker, and from part-time work for Francis Herreshoff as a draftsman when he came back to Gloucester from Detroit in 1952, but the most significant things he took from these short apprenticeships may have been attitudes rather than lessons in structure or mathematics. Lord, Hacker and Herreshoff have all been described as geniuses, and all three were independent men with inventive turns of mind, eccentricities, and an indefinable ability to work through a complex of requirements and possibilities to lines on paper that represented more than a sequence of problems solved.

It would have been a stroke of luck for any student of yacht design to have worked with one of these men; that Bolger worked with all three is extraordinary. And it seems to have been luck—"I went after them," he says, "but it was luck that they held still for it." Yet Bolger claims his brother, Bill, and boatbuilder Nicholas Montgomery as his real mentors. "My brother brought me up to boat design, and taught me to be critical," he says. Nicholas Montgomery, whose boatyard in Gloucester is now run by his son and grandson, with Phil Bolger as in-house designer, was "a thinker and an experimenter," Bolger says. Montgomery was an old school designer/boatbuilder who worked with carved models, and Phil Bolger haunted his yard as a boy. "I used to sit at his feet, and he would lecture me on boat design," the designer says, smiling through his beard at the memory.

Bolger sent a design for a clean-lined 32' sportfisherman to Yachting in the fall of 1951, and it was published in the January, 1952, issue. This first published design elicited "a satisfying amount of correspondence—probably three letters," and it caused Bolger to set up on his own in the house in Gloucester with stock designs for "mostly powerboats, with a few rowboats." None of these early designs showed obvious influence from Lord, Hacker or Herreshoff. The powerboats were lean and angular; the rowing boats—among them the original of the Gloucester Gull rowing dory—were plywood versions of dories and dory skiffs. They were original conceptions, and they were typically simplified in line and structure.

In the middle to late 'fifties, Bolger worked up some production boats, two of which began to make his reputation and one of which tore it down. Bolger freely admits mistakes and disappointments in the boats he designs, and he does it in print. Mistakes are nature's way of telling you you're still learning. He designed the first Striker sportfisherman, and he learned some things about steel construction from the builder. The first Striker was a 24-footer, and Bolger, like Hacker with the Air Force boat, designed a complicated frame structure to be covered with 14-gauge steel. The Nassau-Suffolk Welding Company, which built the boat, used heavier plating for a monocoque structure and dispensed with the framing scheme except to use it as a jig. The hull oilcanned in only a few places during its shakedown run, and "the builder much improved the job," says Bolger. Those first Strikers, with rakish, patrol-boat lines and clean planes of steel and later aluminum, were very beautiful boats. "They didn't sell very well because they didn't run very well," says the designer, "but they looked wonderful."

Bolger had been designing sea-skiff types in the 'fifties, too, and in 1956-57 he designed a carvel-planked 31-footer for Egg Harbor that was a thorough success. "My boast is that it was about two years before any of them came on the used-boat market, and then they sold for more than they had originally." After this, he says, "pride ran before a fall." His friend Terry Kilborne came to him with a scheme "to build boats in Japan where boats can be built cheap." The result was the Out O'Gloucester 30, a "very radical design." It produced what Bolger describes as "the worst day I ever had." When launched, the first of these cruising/fishing powerboats "was 5" down in the stern, wouldn't steer, reached for the moon in trim...Fortunately, Yachting came out that month with an article by Ed Monk on shingles to correct trim problems in powerboats; we did exactly what Monk recommended, and it worked."

Bolger designed powerboats for Striker until the mid-1960s, and at the same time he produced a series of power "dories" and "sampans" for Captain Jim Orrell's Texas Dory Boat Plans. These were dead-simple flatiron/sharpie types in lengths from 15' to 45' for cheap and simple home construction in plywood, and they were exceptionally well-behaved boats despite their shoebox shapes. They were built all over the world—a slick 15-footer as a family boatbuilding project by the keeper of the Eddystone Light in St. Helens, Tasmania; 110 boats from 18' to 30' built by native fishermen on Wallis Island in New Caledonia; hundreds more built by handy and penny-pinching customers in the U.S. A man in Rhode Island wrote Captain Orrell about his Bolger-designed 17' "Sampan Express:" "In rough water, it is unbeatable, and consistently puts the stock boats to shame in both speed and handling. In three-to-five-foot chop, while others are hanging on and hoping, we continue on at ¾ throttle. Surfing down the big ones is quite a thrill, and with the tremendous bow buoyancy no need to worry about digging in."

Bolger's interest in simple boats made from developable materials such as wide planks of pine or sheets of steel, aluminum or plywood goes back to that Masonite boat with the kite sail, although it has been influenced by such academic and/or purposeful exercises as Howard Chapelle's researches into sharpies and the worldwide success of the Texas Dories. Bolger feels that he has had more experience with sharpie types than anybody alive, experience that has included crewing a Star boat for years; owning sailing sharpies, dories and flatiron skiffs for decades; and designing hundreds of plane-sectioned hulls that gave good service. "It's a thing I can do—so I do it," he says, which expresses not half his belief in sharp-form, shallow-draft boats that go together simply and go against the ancient orthodoxy of round sections as the only able form for boats with

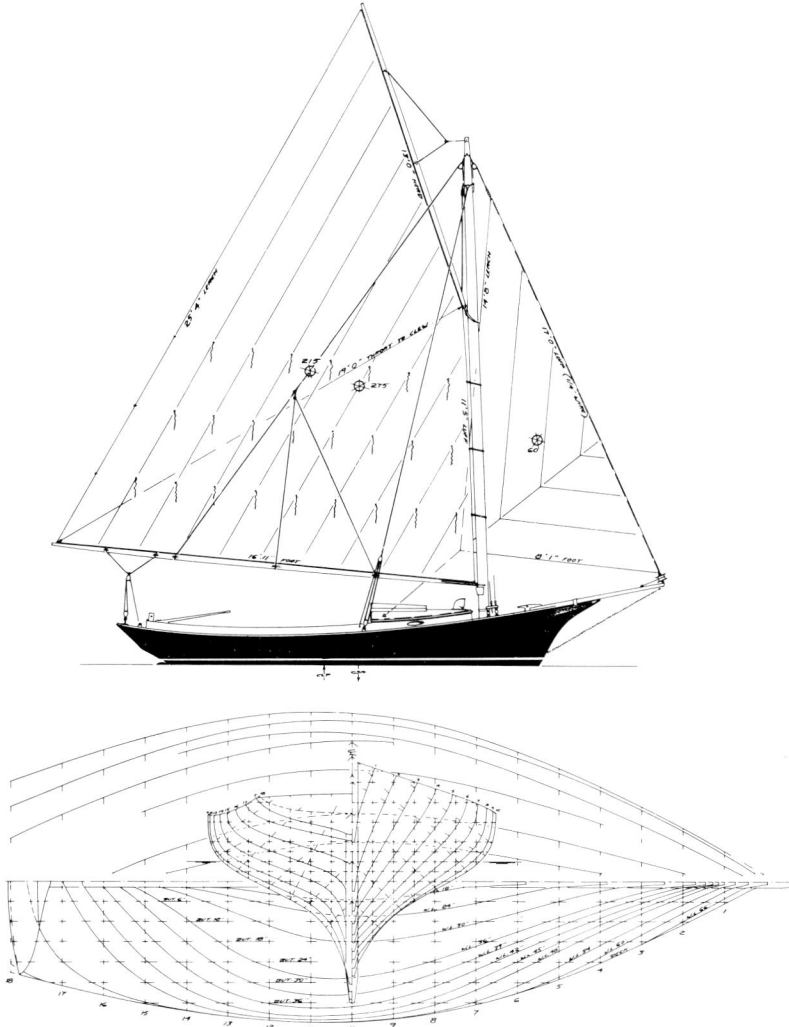

MONHEGAN

"Besides being relatively free of what Claud Worth called 'morbid anxiety about the weather,' a boat of this type has an advantage at the other end of the spectrum: with her deep, easy bow, great momentum, and long-boomed gaff rig, she's much better able to cope with the plague of motorboat wakes in light weather than lighter boats with more modern-looking rigs. As long as she's not pinched, she's a first-class ghoster. She has a very big rig for her size; the size of the boat is so small that such a rig doesn't create any problems in relation to a man's strength, but now and again it will help her surprise some more racy type in light and moderate weather."

—from *Small Boats*

> Bolger is a 1980s-and-beyond sharpie partisan, principally
> because these boats are able to be everyman's yacht, stuck together in the
> backyard from plywood available in the local lumberyard...

seakeeping ability or even comfort in a bay chop.

Sharp-form boats have their own orthodoxy in New England dories, in Chesapeake skipjacks, and in skiffs, garveys and flatirons built for a hundred years from Maine to Florida, where Commodore Ralph Munroe, pal of Nat Herreshoff, was a partisan of the type. Howard I. Chapelle's Smithsonian Bulletin 228 describes them nicely (Chapelle was another partisan) and notes that: "The sharpie's rapid spread in use can be accounted for in its low cost, light draft, speed, handiness under sail, graceful appearance, and rather astonishing seaworthiness... There is a case on record in which a tonging sharpie rescued the crew of a coasting schooner at Branford, Connecticut, during a severe gale, after other boats had proven unable to approach the wreck."

Bolger is a 1980s-and-beyond sharpie partisan, principally because these boats are able to be everyman's yacht, stuck together in the backyard from plywood available in the local lumberyard, and also because their performance can be exciting and their behavior forgiving with proper design. His sharp-form boats have ranged from the elegant *Burgundy* and *Black Skimmer* (shown in these pages) to the *Thomaston Galley* and the controversial *June Bug* (also shown here). *June Bug* recently raised the hackles of a from-the-first-issue subscriber to The Small Boat Journal, who complained of "Phil Bolger's box" and felt that the magazine had "lost sight of the definition of a boat." *June Bug* is definitely a box with a pointy end—"an order of magnitude away," as Bolger might say, from an Edwardian yacht tender of similar volume. But she's a lightweight, stable and useful vehicle as designed, and Bolger anticipated the man's arguments in *30-Odd Boats*, his new book, by commenting on his sharpie purism: "The purist approach results in a very good boat that looks cheap and nondescript. So why not add just a little flare of side and a corresponding rake of stem? Then the sheer could come out of a straight-edged sheet and save at least one long saw cut and possibly a sheet of plywood, i.e., she'd be cheaper as well as 'look more like a boat.' There's an attractive argument that a good boat will look good, and if it doesn't, the designer hasn't made the best of his requirement, or the requirement is too demanding to be prudent. May be. But it also makes me uneasy to deliberately design in something that I'm sure is wrong for the service, and in this case I decided not to do it."

June Bug is a pointed box, but she's a more subtle creation than the amateur flatirons that many of us remember from our first days on the water. She rows nicely, sails tolerably well with her spritsail and leeboard, weighs less than 100 pounds and carries 1000 in calm conditions, and her decked ends enable her to be launched like jetsam from a high-sided vessel without taking on water. She's practical, but she's as ugly as an inflatable by yacht-tender standards. Bolger admits as much, even though he carries an experimental *June Bug* with a pair of dipping lugsails on the deck of his *Resolution*. The letter to Small Boat Journal "really stung," he says, "because it's true." Nevertheless, he believes in both the usefulness of his boxes and their technical credibility. "I started designing boats of a type I was familiar with," he says. "I started designing imitations of things like Amesbury skiffs that were expensive to produce one-off—because they had been designed originally for production. Now I'm getting a better handle on prefabricated shapes—so that I eventually hope to be able to do some very complex shapes...If you can visualize the geometry well enough you can do it, and I think I'll get it if I persist. I don't intend to abandon the boxes."

Harold Payson builds and sells plans for 14 of Bolger's plywood "Instant Boats," some of them the inspired boxes, and all of them able to be built without lofting or jigs in 40 unskilled hours or less. Dynamite Payson's covering letter for these small-boat plans reads like the Charles Atlas ads, and the plain but efficient little boats that result are as satisfying as adding 3″ to the girth of your biceps after a month of Dynamic Tension. Amy Payson keeps albums of photos and letters from pleased home-builders, and Harold says of the boats that "a lot of them look real damned good—they look just like they're supposed to." Harold Payson is a man Phil Bolger describes as "one of those people who don't overwhelm you with brilliance on first acquaintance, but you gradually notice that, whenever you get an opinion out of him, he always turn out to be right. I know two or three other people like that, and I sometimes wonder if civilization doesn't depend on them."

Payson has been building boats for 40 years, ever since his father took an ax to the first one to keep him from being drowned, and he was a commercial lobsterman in South Thomaston, Maine, until 1976. He built traditional bent-oak-and-cedar lobstering skiffs until 1967, the year he built the first of many light dories of Bolger's design. Payson and Bolger have become a perfect, if improbable, team. Bolger is, says Dynamite, "an intense sort of person—I can feel that intensity when he comes up here." Dynamite, despite the nickname, is not an intense sort of person. He is, despite constant interruptions by visitors to his shop, an intense craftsman who produces perfect versions of Bolger's odd but simple ideas for small boats, and he's the test pilot for their rowing and sailing qualities. He's not an automatic believer. "I don't think this thing is going to work at all," he said of an ultra-simplified, multi-chined plywood pram that was the latest Bolger project in midsummer. In mid-August, after he'd named it *Nymph,* tried it out, and decided to call it "the little stick-together boat," he was high in praise of it. "That Bolger is amazing," he said, turning over the shapely little boat he'd painted ivory white, "see here where the frames fit—there are waterways cut in just where the chines have to have tapes of fiberglass all along—you can get them right in there."

Bolger's inventive small boats have a believer in Harold Payson. His larger projects have had a believer for 20 years in Stanley Woodward, an independently wealthy man, and a connoisseur of small yachts, who hired Bolger as the in-house designer for Majorca Yacht and Boat Construction Association (MYABCA), the yard he established in Spain's Balearic Islands. Bolger describes Stanley Woodward as an artist as well as a yachtsman who has the skills to carry clouds of sail on his Bolger-designed boats with the aplomb of a Bully Waterman. Stanley Woodward designed the fanciful sculpture incorporated, á la *Ticonderoga*, into the L. Francis Herreshoff *Bounty* ketches he built in Majorca, and into several Bolger-designed boats built in the Med. Perhaps the most spectacular is *Moccasin*, shown here on pages 72-75.

Moccasin started out with a request from Woodward for a Francis Herreshoff *Nereia* ketch with slightly higher freeboard. By the time Bolger finished thinking the project out, a whole new boat had appeared on paper—a lovely long-keeled hull with shallow draft, big centerboard, a New Haven sharpie's horizontal rudder, and an unstayed cat-yawl rig with a log-canoe topsail and what Bolger describes as "a masthead reaching jib-cum-spinnaker as well." *Moccasin* can set more than 1200 square feet of sail in light air, and she's a fine example of Bolger's eclectic style in rig and his favor for the powerful, low-aspect sailplans which working vessels carried, sometimes as singlehanders, in the past. As Bolger wrote in *30-Odd Boats* in discussing an owner's doubts about a traditionally rigged 20' Tancook whaler type: "I reassured him about the rig, pointing out that the gaff rig was driven out of racing because the Universal and International Rules both penalized large sail area indiscriminately, taking no account of the advantages of rigs whose shape allows the boat to carry more sail without being knocked down. So it came to be taken for granted that a small sail set high was 'more efficient' than a large sail set low. The logic of this, if any, eludes me. I once saw a champion 5.5-meter beaten hull-down by a 50-year-old Massachusetts Bay 18-footer (18-foot waterline, that is). They were both the same length and weight as near as made no odds. The old boat had half again the sail area, but her three-man crew worked less strenuously, with much simpler and cheaper gear, than the same number in the 'modern' boat. If a big rig is cheaper and easier to handle than a small rig, and heels the boat less, I'd be glad to hear somebody try to justify giving the small rig a rating advantage."

Simple, unstayed, low-aspect rigs have been characteristic of Bolger's work over several decades, as well as boats whose hull forms have been designed to be shaped from flat-plane materials. The sharpies and flatties, from the simple boxes to such rakish conceptions as his *Black Skimmer*,

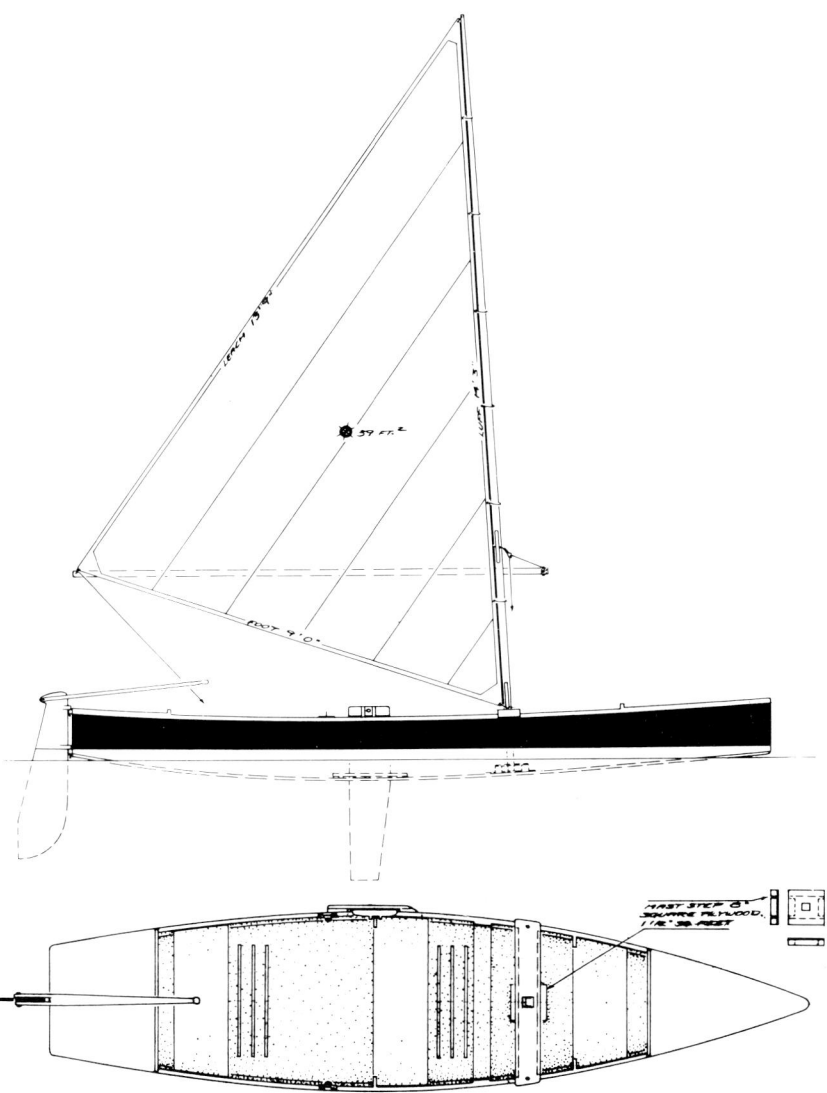

JUNE BUG

"What I wanted was the best compromise available between maximum capacity and stability on minimum overall dimensions and weight, with reasonably good performance under oars. I aimed at 1,000 pounds capacity in quiet conditions, good lines for rowing with up to 400 pounds load, and an empty weight under 100 pounds. The midsection is identical to that of the *Tortoise*, a 6½-foot punt, which has good stability for its weight. I stretched it out to get clean enough lines to row fast around the needed displacement, but no longer than necessary on account of the weight and storage objectives. The 14-foot length selected is arbitrary. A case could be made for a slightly longer boat with less bottom rocker, or a slightly shorter one with more rocker." —from *30-Odd Boats*

> Bolger has designed an amazing range of boats
> that stretch from the 6'5" x 3'2" *Tortoise*, an ingenious rowing/sailing
> box, to the 114'10" replica of the 18th-century warship *Rose*...

cause Bolger some technical doubts in particular but not in general. Sharpie experience, from Commodore Munroe through Howard Chapelle to the owners of Bolger-designed boats that perform and behave well, endorses his faith in the type. "Obviously something with hard corners will have some problems with eddies," he says. "The flat ends, with the jagged angles, make turbulence, so such a boat has to be relatively long...But there's nothing wrong with a square midsection, per se." In a further discussion of hull shape, Bolger says that "a bad type which is long will beat a good type that is short." The Cape Cod catboat, he says, is one of the great conceptions because its midsection is so good that it can be very short and still sail well. The British deep cutter, he says, "is generally a bad type because it has too much displacement for its stability—and, as built, for its buoyancy—and therefore has to be long to perform well." Almost any boat should be flat in the middle, not at either of its ends, he says.

Bolger has designed an amazing range of boats that stretch from the 6'5" x 3'2" *Tortoise*, an ingenious rowing/sailing box, to the 114'10" replica of the 18th-century warship *Rose*, which was built to decorate the Newport, R.I., waterfront. In between have been well-behaved Whitehall boats, Friendship sloops, several ocean-crossing rowing vessels, lobsterboats, a pair of kayaks, deep-draft cruising powerboats, a bone-simple rowing dory, the famous *Folding Schooner* (discussed in NQ14), and fast powerboats that the Italians should be building.

"I love to simplify things," Bolger says of his work. "And I think this is a minority outlook. I think the majority impulse is to make things more complicated." Even this statement is more complicated, the spokesman notwithstanding. Bolger admires the work of a great many other designers—"there are lots," he says. He admires William Garden's designs, "although I disagree with him on a great many technical points." He has an inch-thick sheaf of correspondence with Howard Chapelle in his files. He says he admires Olin Stephens "intensely—basically because he never does anything freakish unless he has to—he's always working back to something recognizable as a boat." Among successful boats, he identifies Bruce Kirby's Laser as "a beautiful example of not trying to revolutionize anything, but just to get it right. It's finished; it's definitive." Bolger feels that Rod Macalpine-Downie's C-Class catamarans also fit his conception of definitive. He identifies Ray Hunt's International 110 as "a very pure conception, but not perhaps definitive...well, close to definitive." He calls Francis Herreshoff's *Bounty* "the most beautiful yacht ever designed or built—a flamboyant thing with a riot of sweeping, twisting, converging curves, all set off with intricate detail and ornament, all blending into a perfectly traditional effect overall." He judges the Gokstad ship "perhaps the most advanced wooden structure ever created by man."

Bolger has an intense personal and professional involvement with definitive. It is a thing he's been thinking about all his life, but with an independent point of view he once wrote about in these pages in discussing Francis Herreshoff: "L.F.H. thought himself a lesser man than his father...He had no hesitation in imitating his father's designs (but never those of Burgess). More often, though, there is hardly a trace of his father's influence; the designs reflect an entirely different line of thought. It's surely remarkable that after 27 years of exposure to such a man as Nathanael Herreshoff, Francis Herreshoff remained so tranquil in mind that he strained neither to be like his father nor to be different."

Phil Bolger is like that. His work—influenced by mentors like Lord, Hacker, Herreshoff, Nick Montgomery and Bill Bolger, and inspired perhaps by the likes of Garden, Hunt and Stephens—is very much his own. It is nearly 450 different boats thusfar, nearly all different from the work of others, and nearly all different from one another. Bolger once designed a radical plywood daysailer for a sail-training scheme—a 21' x 5'6" progenitor of the *Folding Schooner* with sponsons along the topsides for reserve buoyancy, three spritsails with spars light enough for boys to unship, leeboards, plenty of room to sprawl around, and plywood carpentry straightforward enough for high-school woodworking shops. The sponsor of the project took the drawings to a number of people, including what Bolger describes in *Small Boats* as "a very distinguished yacht designer." "They one and all told him that the design was a disastrously bad one, would be slow and clumsy, and would quickly break up. They also told him that Bolger was notoriously irresponsible; wild ideas like this, they told him, were what you got if you didn't hold his nose tightly down on some safe and sane standard." The design was eventually built by another client, and Bolger reports that "she proved a lively sailer, though wet." She had no structural problems. As he wrote of the project in *Small Boats:* "What they say about me has this much truth: I do love unusual and extreme boats, and I was tickled at the thought of the outrage the design would cause and how it would be silenced when she was tried."

Editor's Note: There are 136 of Phil Bolger's designs shown—and described in the designer's delightful prose—in four books published by International Marine Publishing Company—*Small Boats, The Folding Schooner and Other Adventures in Boat Design, Different Boats* and *30-Odd Boats*. Plans for many of his rowing, sailing and powered dories and dory skiffs are available from Texas Dory Boat Plans, P.O. Box 720, Galveston, Texas 77553. Plans for 14 "Instant Boats," from the 6'5" *Tortoise* punt to the 31' *Folding Schooner*, are available from Harold H. Payson & Co., Pleasant Beach Road, South Thomaston, Maine 04858.

Jim Melcher sails his Alert in her home waters on Cape Cod at left and right. Below right is her ample owner's stateroom with its bookshelves and double-sized berth. Melcher lives aboard this 33′6″ x 7′8″ boat, and he's already sailed her 5000 miles in cruises on the Atlantic coast. Future plans include a highway trip to Seattle for cruising from Puget Sound to Alaska, a winter in the Caribbean in 1983-84, and the possibility of shipping her to Europe as deck cargo on a freighter for further adventures in the French and Dutch canals.

ALERT

Jim Melcher has traveled nearly 5000 miles in this unusual leeboard-equipped cruising ketch since she was built in the summer of 1981, and as this is written he's in the Bahamas enjoying places that Alert's draft of less than 2′ can carry him into. Phil Bolger calls this design Manatee, and he designed her for a syndicate of six cruising yachtsmen who wanted a 33′ hull of extreme shoal draft with good cabin and cockpit space. Melcher's Alert is the prototype, and thus far the only one completed.

In Different Boats, Bolger describes the evolution of the high-freeboard hull: "She's derived from Thames barges, which actually had hard chines and a perfectly rectangular midship section, but she's stretched out much finer forward than a barge ever was. It's been said that barge-type hulls can't stand a fine bow, but that's only true if the fineness is carved out of the long mid-body they need to sail on. In this hull, it's been added on, making her four or five feet longer than a blunt-bowed barge model of similar capacity."

The boxy shape of Alert's midsection makes for a generous 12′ x 7′ main cabin with two settee berths, galley counter, two hanging lockers, and a collection of bins, bookshelves and other stowage. Forward is an owner's stateroom with a big double berth. The original design had a 4′ x 6′ pop-top for full headroom over the galley, but Jim Melcher has added a trunk cabin which Bolger considers ugly. Melcher lives on Alert full-time, in New England in the summer and in Florida and elsewhere for the rest of the year, and full headroom is a convenience.

Melcher's previous boat, Triumph, was a 36′ "Old Glory" leeboard ketch designed by Pete Culler. "This boat sails rings around Triumph," he says, and he's pleased with her behavior at sea. On the way south this past fall he left Shinnecock Inlet on Long Island for a straight shot to Cape May, estimating it would take 36 hours. The wind picked up to 30+ and he made the passage in 24 hours, running before it with three reefs in the main and no mizzen. "When the seas lengthened out more, she was surging down them—surfing almost," he says. Alert handled with no vices, he reports, and took no water on deck.

Now retired, Melcher plans to spend this winter in the Bahamas and the Florida Keys. With hull dimensions of 33′6″ x 7′8″, Alert is trailerable without special permits, and he expects to take her to Seattle on the highway in the spring. Melcher spent ten years in the Pacific Northwest as a boatbuilder and salmon fisherman after World War II, and he looks forward to revisiting his old territory, cruising Puget Sound and eventually sailing north to visit his son and grandson in Alaska.

Melcher plans to be in the Caribbean in the winter of 1983-84 with Alert, and someday he would like to ship her to Europe for further adventures in the French and Dutch canals.

TASHTEGO

An altogether rakish conception, this daysailing and weekending sharpie that Phil Bolger calls *Black Skimmer* seems to be one of the designer's favorites. Bolger's eyes light up and his voice shifts into a higher gear when he talks about her. "Everybody who has one of those boats loves it," he says, as he tries to remember all the places where they've been built—Florida, Puget Sound, New Zealand, Zimbabwe.

The boat shown here was built by the Old Wharf Dory Company in Wellfleet on Cape Cod, and she spends her summers in Pleasant Bay when she's not exploring the thin backwaters of the Cape or venturing south to Vineyard Sound. "We've sailed her all over the place," says her owner Drew McManus, describing weekend outings, an annual cruise of three or four weeks, even after-dinner sails on weeknights. McManus and his wife Barbara named their boat *Tashtego* after Melville's Indian harpooneer, and they like her a lot. Former offshore sailors, and owners of previous boats that included one of Bolger's *Dovekies*, a 25′ Tancook-whaler type built by Peter VanDine, and a 28′ Scandinavian sloop designed by Aage Utzon, they find *Tashtego* a package full of simple pleasures. "She's the most enjoyable of all the boats we've had—for our purposes. We enjoy sailing close to shore where we can hear the songbirds...and it's nice to be able to step out of the boat in three inches of water in some interesting place."

This boat is a rare synthesis of Bolger's unorthodox ideas—sharpie hull, unstayed flexing masts with sprit booms, very little draft, and two leeboards. Of leeboards, Bolger writes in *The Folding Schooner*...: "Perhaps this is as good a place as any to run through the answers to the standard questions about leeboards: no, they don't have to be handled every tack—leave them both down all the time; no, don't build them asymmetrical or toed-in, you'll overdo it if you try it at all; yes, they're noisy and collect driftwood and pot-warp; yes, they do need to be that big and especially that wide, and they also need at least that much ballast; yes, I agree that they're ugly." *Tashtego's* leeboards permit her to sail to windward effectively and to float in 10″ of water, and they use up no space in a cuddy cabin that Drew McManus describes as "very ergonometrically designed."

This boat was built with marine plywood, WEST epoxy and one-piece spruce spars three years ago for about $15,000, including sails. The designer thinks that her professionally-built price today would vary between $11,000 and $15,000, depending upon materials, and that a backyard builder could do the job for about $5,000.

Built by a professional shop on Cape Cod for Drew McManus of Chatham, Massachusetts, *Tashtego* is Phil Bolger's 25′3″ x 7′ Black Skimmer design, an overnighting and daysailing sharpie that draws 3′6″ with her leeboards down and floats in 10″ of water with them up. Barbara and Drew McManus sail this boat nearly every day in the summer, and use her for coastal cruises of as much as a month. The cuddy cabin shown here is snug but serviceable, and the owner describes *Tashtego* as "pretty darned comfortable" even on voyages of some duration. For daysailing the shoal waters behind the Cape, exploring wild marshes and sandy islands, and anchoring out without another boat in sight, says McManus, she's unbeatable.

INSTANT BOATS

Harold "Dynamite" Payson smiles from the lower corner of the opposite page, and smiling in their own way elsewhere are four of the 14 Instant Boats that Phil Bolger has designed for ultra-simple home construction in plywood. A lot of Bolger's work during the past 30 years has been boats designed for amateur builders— a venerable tradition that began in the U.S. with Charles G. Davis designs published in Rudder in the 1890s, passed through the design-every-month work of Bill Atkin in Motor Boating for nearly 40 years until the late 1950s, and included boats from the drawing boards of Sam Rabl, Weston Farmer, Viktor Harasty, John Atkin and Glen L. Witt, among many others. Some build-'em-yourself boats have accomplished more than others—the Star Boat began as a cheap one-design for amateur construction, and a 28′ sloop of Viktor Harasty's crossed the North Atlantic to enter the OSTAR and sailed back from Plymouth to Newport—but every one of perhaps thousands of home-building designs has been a noble effort to bring a useful little yacht to a man or woman who wanted a boat but couldn't afford to have someone else build it.

Four of Phil Bolger's and Harold Payson's "Instant Boats" are shown on these pages: the new little *Nymph* pram at far left, the Pointy Skiff at center, the *Tortoise* pram on this page, and the *Kotick* kayak below left. Plans for the 6'5" *Tortoise* and 12' *Kotick* are $10; plans for the 8' *Nymph* and the 10'6" Pointy Skiff are $15. All are designed for ultra-simple and relatively unskilled construction in plywood with no lofting of lines or building of jigs required. Lines from the plans are drawn on the plywood sheets, parts are cut out with a sabre saw, and the project proceeds with marine glue, brass screws and/or Anchorfast nails. And if the home-boatbuilder gets in trouble he can call Harold Payson for advice. These are boats that Bolger describes as "cheap and expendable," but they make for fine tenders, kids' boats or vehicles for basic fooling around on the water. Amateur craftsmen do well with them, according to Dynamite Payson. "A lot of them look real damned good—they look just like they're supposed to," he says.

These four are basic boats—the boxy *Tortoise* about as basic as you can get—but they are carefully planned to go together in 40 hours or less, to be made from materials available in the local lumberyard, and to require ordinary household tools and skills. The drawing-board work is Bolger's, and the building, refining and testing work is Harold Payson's responsibility. Bolger describes himself as "not a very good boatbuilder." Dynamite Payson is a good boatbuilder, experienced in plank-on-frame and cedar-on-oak ribbed construction.

Harold Payson sells plans for all 14, answers the telephone cheerfully to questions from customers, keeps photo albums of amateur-built Instant Boats, and—when time permits—builds them for sale. The professional builder gets the same kicks from these projects as his amateur customers do—"the special satisfaction of commanding your own handiwork on the water, and being proud of it," as the letter that accompanies the plan sheets promises.

These boats are simple—and relatively instant—but not unsophisticated. Bolger describes his 12' *Kotick* kayak, shown here with the designer aboard, as one of the best things he's ever done. And the new little *Nymph* pram, upper left with Dynamite in command, is designed so that right-angle cuts in the plywood assume the proper bevels when the sides and bottom pieces fit together. Plans for 14 Instant Boats, from the 31' Folding Schooner to the 6'5" *Tortoise*, are available at prices from $30 to $10 from Harold H. Payson & Co., Pleasant Beach Rd., South Thomaston, Maine 04858.

Built in Mallorca in 1974, Stanley Woodward's *Moccasin* was shipped to Virginia in the spring of 1982, and sailed the lower Chesapeake last summer as a daysailer and occasional overnighter. Inspired by the dolphins that Francis Herreshoff designed into the rails of *Ticonderoga*, Woodward designed the handsome seahorse shown here as a rudder ornament for *Moccasin*. She's a thoroughly original conception, from the seahorse forward to her clipper bow.

MOCCASIN

In an article several years ago in Woodenboat titled "Moccasin—Whose Time Has Come," Stanley Woodward described his boat's pre-design conversations: "I wanted an easily-handled vessel whose speed would not be handicapped by any rating rule. In particular, I insisted that the boat be so well-balanced sailing on the wind, or running, that no awkward self-steering apparatus attached to the stern should be necessary. I also wanted the boat to have sufficient sail area to eliminate the need for an auxiliary engine." Bolger talked his client into a slow-turning 8-hp Stuart Turner auxiliary with a Luke feathering propeller, but otherwise Stanley Woodward got the cruising and daysailing yawl he wanted.

Moccasin's hull, whose design began with a look at Francis Herreshoff's *Nereia* and soon went elsewhere, is a long-bodied, easy-lined form with a clipper bow, slightly hollow entry, long horizontal keel, upswept buttock lines and an elongated rudder reminiscent of the New Haven sharpies. She's a canoe form in profile, but beamy enough at 36'9" x 9'10" that her beam is much of her ballast, supplemented by 2700 pounds of lead in the keel, and helped to windward by a centerboard that drops to 7' from her board-up draft of 2'.

She was built in Mallorca in 1974 by the owner and two Spanish fishboat builders, and she has a strong hull of 1"-thick African mahogany planking on sawn frames of hard pine and a keel of iroko, with Everdur bronze fastenings throughout and with teak and mahogany trim. Below decks are two simple cabins—a pair of pipe berths and a portable head forward, main cabin with a pair of berth-sized seats, chart table, hanging locker and simple galley—which gain athwartships space from the raised-deck design but have less than standing headroom. Woodward has owned more conventional yachts—the 56' *Belisarius* designed by Francis Herreshoff and the William-Fife-designed 33' sloop *Nayatonga* —but *Moccasin*'s accommodations suit him fine. As he wrote in Woodenboat: "*Moccasin* is the first boat I have owned without standing headroom everywhere below. It was, therefore, surprising to me that the lack of headroom has actually made the saloon appear more attractive. Proportions are certainly better, and since no attempt was made to crowd the interior I have not lived with a better arrangement."

Moccasin's most radical feature is her unstayed rig with sprit booms, an arrangement that evolved from Bolger's experience with his *Dovekie* and *Black Skimmer* designs, among others, and from Woodward's historical perspective. The owner cites some of the Chesapeake workboats and Virginia pilot schooners of the last century as examples of relatively large vessels with unstayed spars, along with log canoes, from which *Moccasin* borrowed her big square topsail.

The self-tending, balanced jib was Woodward's addition (Bolger was in favor of a cat yawl rig), and the designer suggested the full-battened mizzen, which can be left set a lot of the time to steady the hull at anchor or on a mooring. "For an impulsive daysail," Bolger writes in *The Folding Schooner...*, "one has only to haul on the main halyard and cast off the mooring pennant." *Moccasin*'s mainmast must support nearly 1200 sq. ft. of sail at times, and its structure is thick-walled spruce with graphite fiber and WEST epoxy applied at the joints.

Stanley Woodward describes *Moccasin* as "a terrific daysailer." She's slippery, among other things, and Woodward relishes the tale of the 14-mile, triangular-course race she won in Mallorca against ¾-ton and 1-ton boats with racing crews. In light, variable air, she finished 14 minutes, 35 seconds ahead.

The latest of more than a half-dozen 25′ outboard launches that Phil Bolger has designed during three decades, *TarTar* is intended for lightweight cold-molded construction, and she keeps the high, clipper-profile bow and rakish windshield of her predecessors. She's one more of Bolger's "different boats," and she's another Stanley Woodward commission. She's also a successful variation on a theme—the all-purpose open outboard for fishing and overnight cruising—that has scores of heavier fiberglass examples in the marketplace.

This boat is an elite version of the type, custom-built and priced at about $23,000. "She's perfect...There's nothing we would want to do to change her," says Stanley Woodward, who uses *TarTar* in the lower Chesapeake "for just about everything—as a launch, to cross the Bay in 25 minutes instead of an hour and a half by car, for fishing, to get to New Point Light Island, a place we like that looks just like the Bahamas..."

The skinny hull with well-flared topsides forward—25′6″ x 22′ x 6′10″—knocks down spray effectively, and the loaded weight of about 2400 pounds on a long, flat-at-the-transom, soft-chined hull permits Woodward's 90-hp Evinrude to drive her at 30 knots top and 24 knots cruising.

This boat is not roomy, but she's a comfortable camping-out vehicle, and a fine day boat with a large cockpit and a soft top to shelter the two padded bench seats forward. In the cuddy cabin are a forepeak compartment large enough for a portable head, and the bench seats become full-size berths with 5″ cushions. The two seats aft of the cabin door will seat guests comfortably on day trips, and a sliding bench across the cockpit can be used at the helm console or at the transom.

This elegant, versatile powerboat was built by Zimmerman Marine, Miles, VA 23114, from four layers of ⅛″ western red cedar laid in WEST-System epoxy and covered with 10-ounce fiberglass cloth. *TarTar* is the first of what Steve Zimmerman hopes will be a few sisters, and he says he's hoping for a customer who wants one finished bright.

TARTAR

Another "different boat" commissioned by Stanley Woodward, *TarTar* is an all-purpose 25′ outboard launch with a roomy cockpit, a pair of bench seats behind the windshield, and a forepeak compartment that accommodates a portable head. The bench seats are 6′5″, fitted with 5″-thick cushions, and double as overnight berths sheltered by a soft-top system. The 2400-pound hull planes at 14 knots and hits 30 knots with a 90-hp outboard.

DOVEKIE

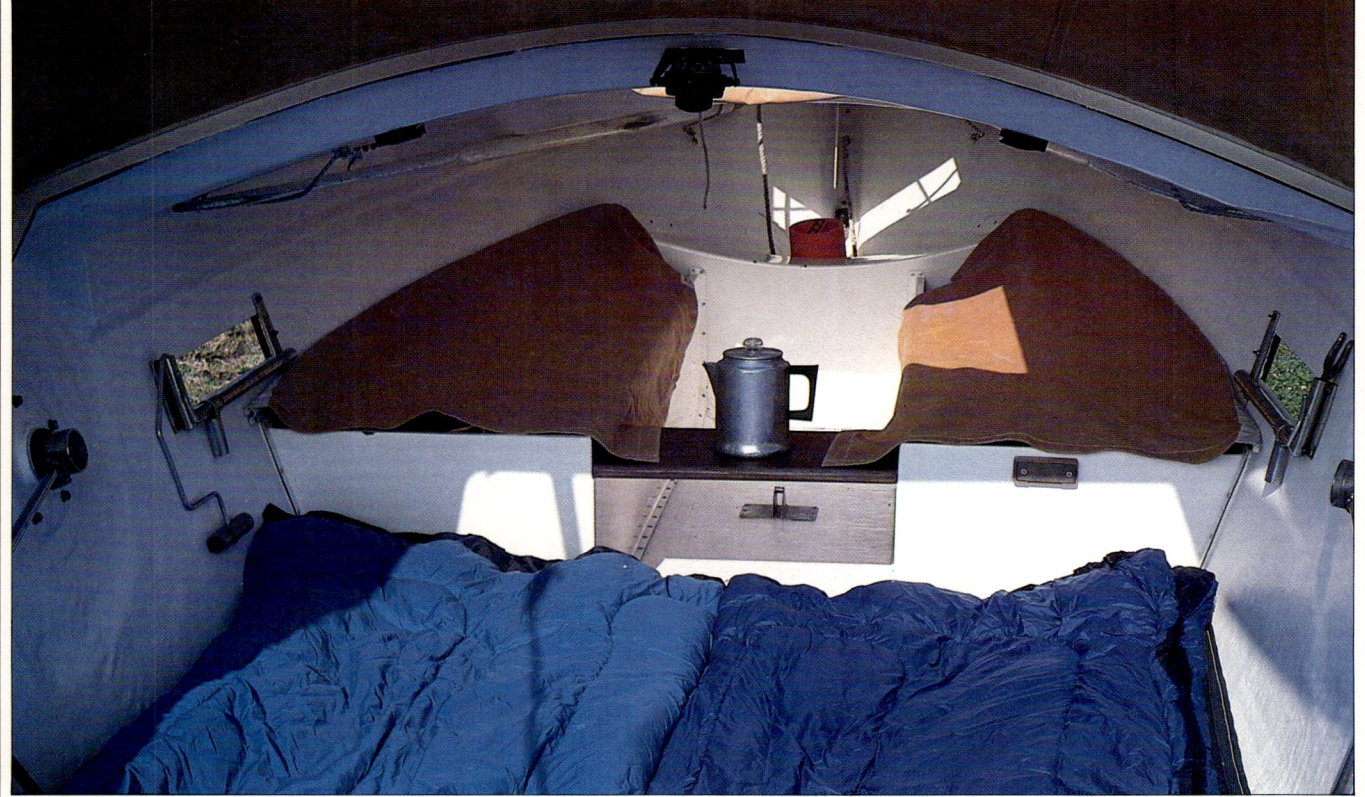

Peter Duff has built 64 of these rowing/sailing/trailering/camping-out cruisers during the past four years at his Edey & Duff yard in Mattapoisett, Massachusetts, and although Phil Bolger drew her lines the boat has been a spirited and creative collaboration. "It is as much Peter's work as mine," says Bolger.

The first *Dovekie* was built as a one-off for Bolger himself. The designer sailed her up to Gloucester that spring, then cruised south in June to Mystic Seaport's famous Small Boat Workshop, where she caused quite a stir. Two years later, Bolger talked his friend the fiberglass boatbuilder into a production run. Peter Duff wishes he were building more of them, but he's happy with what he and Bolger have wrought. What Duff calls "an absolutely trouble-free boat" is a birdlike barge of a vehicle that weighs only 600 pounds and trailers with as little trouble as an outboard runabout, sails efficiently with two leeboards and 143 sq. ft. of sail on a freestanding portable spar, rows smoothly with two to four sweeps, and brings her crew into the watery wilderness with plenty of sheltered space for overnighting in sleeping bags.

The operative word here may be wilderness, for the whole idea of this "beach cruiser" is to enjoy places where conventional boats don't go. Next summer, Duff and a coterie of *Dovekie* customers and friends expect to cruise from Cape Charles north to Chincoteague on the Atlantic side of the Delmarva Peninsula—"wild territory which few sailing people ever see." This will be what Duff calls "the magnum opus" of the *Dovekie* cruising season. Previous cruises have visited New Brunswick's St. John River, the North Channel of Lake Huron, and the Bras d'Or Lakes of Nova Scotia. There is also an annual Chesapeake cruise in the spring and a long-weekend cruise in the Northeast in early summer.

Peter and Margaret Duff have enjoyed all of these adventures aboard the boat shown here, and they have noticed how their drive-there-and-camp-out-on-the-water cruising style appeals not only to younger outdoors types but to older yachtsmen. "We're enjoying it very much," Duff says, "and we have quite a number of owners in their fifties and sixties—people who've owned larger boats and are scaling themselves down for various reasons. They tell me they're cruising to places they never thought they'd get to see."

The *Dovekie* hull draws only 4", but its fiberglass-and-Airex structure is nearly an inch thick on the bottom. The 1982 price is $6190, and it includes "everything you'd need to cruise except the trailer—lifejackets, flare kit, ground tackle, ash oars, everything..."

NAUTICAL QUARTERLY

The rowing, sailing and camping-out cruising capabilities of Phil Bolger's and Peter Duff's *Dovekie* are indicated in these few photographs. She was created for no-frills, no-hassles cruising and, with her light trailering weight and 4" boards-up draft, for easy access to a variety of cruising grounds by highway and shoal-water gunkholing when she arrives. Peter Duff and his wife Margaret have put her to the test during the past four years with cruises in Florida, the Great Lakes, New England, Chesapeake Bay, and Canada's Maritime Provinces.

LOA: 21'5"
LWL: 19'
Beam: 6'8"
Draft: 4" (boards up) 30" (boards down)
Weight: 600 pounds
Sail Area: 143 sq. ft.
Hull: Hand-layup fiberglass with Airex foam core
Price: $6190
Builder: Edey & Duff, 26 Harbor Rd., Mattapoisett, MA 02739

FOOLS RUSH IN WHERE ANGLERS FEAR TO TREAD

BY DAVID FINKELSTEIN AND JACK LONDON

The down payment on our marlin was only $18,000. Other substantial installments would follow, of course, but we were pleased to have started modestly. Besides, hadn't we decided to participate in tournaments and tie into trophy fish? Why concern ourselves with the unsporting matter of money? "We'll take it in cash," we whispered to the bank manager that morning in Key West, America's own Banana Republic. "Twenty-dollar bills, and you can put them in here," said Phil Caputo, hefting an attaché case. □ The manager arched an eyebrow. Phil's jokes about himself had been on the mark—he did look like a Mafia hit man from Chicago. The manager looked cynically at the rest of us as we shifted uneasily. We were properly nervous about carrying all that cash up the Keys. Lugging large sums of money around South Florida could lead three innocent fishermen to "take a mort," as Phil's imaginary Windy City hit man might have put it.

Unlike the Hemingway characters who had robbed this same bank in *To Have and Have Not*, we were waving Dreyfus Liquid Assets Checks, not guns. But the request for cash had aroused the manager's suspicions. "Another Key West drug deal," she must have been thinking as she took the attaché case and strolled off to fill it with money. When she returned a few minutes later her initial dismay had become indignation. Handing Phil the case as though it contained atomic waste, she waved us to a nearby counting room. Our little drama at the bank concluded, we drove up the Keys and paid for our new boat. Thus began our adventures with *Candide*, so named because of her new owners' boundless optimism and their conviction that everything would always turn out for the best.

After searching all spring for a Bertram 31 sportfisherman, we had located one finally in Islamorada. She was an older boat, but loaded with the sort of big-game paraphernalia that sends ardent fishermen into fits of ecstasy: Lee outriggers, a fishfinder and depth recorder, Pompanette fighting chair with adjustable back and leg positions, and much more. Best of all, on the starboard side of the cockpit, just behind the cabin, was a stainless-steel gin pole that would bring the trophy catches of our dreams over the gunwale and into the cockpit with us.

The boat was in rough shape when we first saw her. One of her outriggers was badly bent, the result of an encounter with an undrawn drawbridge. Her rubrails had served their function admirably—what hadn't already been rubbed away was hanging off. The seats that had once been mounted on the deck of her flying bridge had come unstuck and were stowed in the forward cabin. The teak work was bleached white by sun and saltwater. She was a mess; but we didn't care. She was a Bertram 31, after all, and we probably would have bought her even if she had had no stern. The price had been quickly agreed upon, the owner's only stipulation being that we hand over cash.

With the purchase of *Candide*, Caputo and London were saddled with the daily routine of getting up early each morning for the two-hour trip from Key West to Islamorada, there to spend long days cleaning, repairing and refitting the boat. Every day they slaved away in the late-spring sun until, exhausted by work and heat, they stumbled to the car and returned to the Island City. Often on the way back they would fall into Jose's Cantina on Summerland Key and, on partnership funds, refresh themselves with heaping plates of Jewfish steaks accompanied by black beans and rice and washed down with potent Cuban coffee.

In six weeks the boat experienced a gradual but noticeable metamorphosis. Even the teak had been cleaned and oiled. Then came the word that initiated the great adventure: The U.S. had lifted its travel restrictions, and the Cuban government, desperate for hard currency, had decided not only to sponsor a marlin tournament but also to invite Americans to participate. Here was an opportunity for glory. *Candide*, her masters, and a select few who would join them, would show the Cubans, as Hemingway had before them, how the noble marlin was stalked and conquered. What did it matter that none of us knew a thing about marlin fishing? We would learn.

Candide was readied for action. After weighing the qualifications of the many who wanted to share the adventure with us, we chose our crew. They were selected, or so it seemed, on the basis of their inexperience and inability to make a positive contribution. Garrett Anger, a Fire Island clamdigger who fished for sharks and bluefish on summer weekends, was recruited from the north to skipper the boat despite his full ignorance of southern waters. It didn't matter that he knew as little as we did about billfish, or that he would be competing with some of the savviest marlin fishermen and best-equipped boats in America and Cuba. Standing 6'7", Garrett looked like a charter captain, and he knew everything about starting the engines. And if one of us brought a fish close aboard, he was powerful enough to reach over the covering boards and drag it in with his bare hands.

The privilege of serving as mate was bestowed upon Dick Stammers, whose primary qualification was that he worked in a Key West tackle shop from which we hoped to borrow equipment. He knew even less about marlin than Garrett, but he assured us that he could tie important fishing knots such as the Bimini twist, and best of all that he knew one or two ways to rig baits for trolling. On themselves, the owners of *Candide* conferred the distinction of being The Three Anglers. The ideal Angler should have a strong back, enjoy being cursed and harangued by a captain, and have no idea what he's doing. Except for strong backs, the Three Anglers filled the bill almost perfectly.

The sixth member of the crew, selected as official photographer, was

---

Candide was readied for action.
After weighing the qualifications of the
many who wanted to share
the adventure with us, we chose
our crew. They were selected, or so it
seemed, on the basis of their
inexperience...

Bob Eber, vice-president of a large Wall Street brokerage firm. Bob boasted appropriate photographic credentials: he had taken hundreds of acceptable snapshots of his family with a Kodak Instamatic, and he had recently supplied himself with a new camera at a local flea market. *Candide's* trip across the Straits of Florida was planned in fine detail. We spent an intense hour the evening before departure poring over the charts and working out a course to Havana. The six of us each had a go at it, and five different courses were recommended. We wisely chose the one on which Anger and Caputo seemed to agree. Nor did we neglect the marlin. The afternoon before departure, having driven from TV store to TV store, we finally found a video machine at the Florida Keys Community College Library. There, glued to our seats, we studied an hour-long tape on marlin fishing off Australia's Great Barrier Reef which we had borrowed from the public relations people at Qantas Airways. "So that's how they do it," muttered Garrett Anger every few minutes, pretending he understood. "But I can't really make out how they rig their baits," complained Stammers, squinting at the screen until we thought he should put on his sunglasses. "Good photography," said Bob Eber.

The following morning, *Candide* and her crew left Key West in high excitement after topping off the fuel tanks. Many other boats were making the passage from Key West in a group, but *Candide* was not a vessel that moved with the herd. The 90-mile crossing was uneventful. Occasionally we spotted other fishermen in the distance, but for the most part it was a solitary passage. Early in the afternoon, Phil saw smoke in the distance, and shortly the Cuban coast appeared on the horizon. As we closed the shore, a grey-painted, Soviet-built gunboat, silhouetted against the Havana skyline, turned, accelerated rapidly, and bore down on us throwing a roostertail astern. We hoped we were expected. The gunboat slowed, and an English-speaking voice informed us through a loud-hailer that we had missed our destination, the small harbor of Barlovento, by some 20 miles to the west. Directing us to follow, the Cubans raced off in a southwesterly direction. Indignant but undaunted, Garrett rammed the throttles forward and we screamed along, the two barrels of both carburetors chugging fuel. "I'll catch that bastard," Garrett shouted as the gunboat, with its thousands of horsepower, quickly became a speck in the distance.

As we neared Barlovento, a small red speedboat powered by a Yamaha outboard came out to meet us, and the man aboard gestured us toward shore. Just then, *Candide's* engines sputtered and stopped dead. Even Garrett couldn't start them, and it occurred to one of us to check the fuel tanks. Sure enough, there wasn't a drop. Yet according to our calculations, there should have been 20-odd gallons remaining—more than enough to have made the crossing without mishap. Employing a combination of fractured Spanish and gestures that would have done credit to Marcel Marceau, Bob Eber managed to convey our trouble to the baffled speedboat pilot. Finally understanding, he threw a line to the drifting *Candide,* and towed six embarrassed Americans to a fuel dock, passing a gauntlet of sportfishing machines whose size and posh made us cringe all the more. *Candide's* tanks only took 150 gallons; the careful Caputo had thought their capacity was 180. "Hemingway must have run out of gas once in a while, too," said Phil.

Demonstrating a remarkable ability to put humiliating experiences aside as though they happened every day, we moved to the slip where Cuban customs officials were checking passports and visas. As we waited, a Cuban frogman jumped off the pier and swam under our boat. At first we imagined that he was checking to see if we had remembered to attach our propellers, but we watched him swim under other boats and realized that it was nothing personal. Although we alone looked too incompetent to be counter-revolutionaries, it seems that every boat was subject to a search for hidden explosives. Once customs was cleared and dollars converted to pesos, the four of us who were to stay ashore took a taxi into Havana. Garrett and Dick stayed aboard, and set to work preparing for the next day's practice fishing.

We were lucky to catch a taxi. Appropriately known as *Los Incapturables,* Havana taxi drivers prefer not to stop to pick up passengers. "Why should we?" our driver explained. "We make our salaries regardless." We couldn't argue with him. The ride into Havana took about 20 minutes. We wished it had taken longer. The driver had the mind-set of a kamikaze pilot. Fortunately, traffic was light. The few cars on the streets—old Kaisers, Packards, Studebakers and other relics of the 'forties—were as hell-bent as our cab, all propelled by men like Hudson's chauffeur in *Islands in the Stream,* who "was an excellent car handler with beautiful reflexes in the illogical and neurotic Cuban traffic."

The drive into Havana took us along Fifth Avenue and other legendary residential boulevards, but the city looked like Palm Beach become the

---

Appropriately known as
Los Incapturables, Havana taxi drivers
prefer not to stop to pick
up passengers. "Why
should we?" our driver explained. "We
make our salaries
regardless..."

South Bronx. Once-elegant homes were falling into ruin after decades of neglect by post-revolutionary tenants—mostly students and migrants from the countryside. The ornate facades were crumbling, and once-manicured gardens were wild with tropical foliage. A pervasive air of melancholy, the reverse of its old vibrancy, hung over Havana; the city had literally gone to seed, its mansions and churches now only decaying monuments to a vanished way of life. Like most socialist cities, Havana is now little more than a bureaucratic center, urban but not urbane. In fact, it seemed downright provincial—but, then again, so did we upstart fishermen from the States.

Our taxi shot along the Malecon, Havana's shoreline drive, until we reached the Hotel Riviera, where we were to sleep for the next week. Built in the 1950s by Americans, and primarily for Americans, it now provided refuge for a variety of travelers, including a number of dour, dark-suited Russians who prowled about the lobby and seemed as out of place as polar bears in the tropics. Our rooms looked out over mountains and ocean, and we watched handline fishermen work the edge of the Gulf Stream just a few hundred yards offshore, where "the great blue river," as Hemingway called it, passed close by the city, its depth dropping suddenly from 100 to 600 fathoms, and its color darkening dramatically from azure to indigo.

The event that had brought us here was billed as the Blue Marlin International Tourist Tournament, a followup to the Hemingway Tournament held a few months before. The tournament, in truth, was neither international nor touristic. One token Cuban boat entered the competition. The remaining 29 were American. The multimillion-dollar U.S. flotilla that so incongruously descended upon the Socialist Republic of Cuba had been haphazardly recruited by a couple of now-absent Florida entrepreneurs whose relationship with the Cuban authorities no one understood.

The morning after our arrival we began fishing, experimenting with different baits to see which were effective. The options included cero mackerel, grey mullet, bonita, horse balao, squid, and a few small dolphin—a variety sufficient to tempt any billfish interested in a balanced diet. But all the baits we had brought from Florida were frozen, and they didn't look particularly appetizing even to us. Fishing with only two rods, we selected a sad-looking cero mackerel and a mullet, and put them out on either side of the bright blue-and-white teaser that swam about 60' astern. *Candide* ran zigzag patterns back and forth across the flow of the Gulf Stream, working her way eastward toward Morro Castle. Miraculously, both baits trolled beautifully through water that was fouled with refuse. Skimming the surface of an easy sea, they resembled wounded fish struggling on their sides. For a change we seemed to be doing something right.

As expectantly as little boys after bullheads, The Three Anglers rotated hourly shifts in the fighting chair. Each waited impatiently for his chance while Garrett kept the time on a watch he borrowed from Bob Eber. As the morning wore on, however, our eagerness gave way to ennui. A few hours of staring at the water in hopes of seeing signs of fish had us hallucinating at every ripple and shouting false alarms until, growing weary, we began dozing off in the heat of the famous mid-day sun. But early in the afternoon, when it was Phil's turn to doze in the chair, we were galvanized by Dick Stammers, posted as lookout on the flying bridge, and too concerned about the performance of his frozen baits to sleep, who shouted that magic word: marlin! We awoke with a start to see a fish slashing in from the starboard side at terrific speed, its dorsal fin clearing the water. When it reached the bait, its head lifted and its bill slammed into our woebegone mackerel. The outrigger pin released, giving the fish a short dropback, and Garrett, remembering the Qantas videotape, put both throttles ahead in Australian fashion, allowing the forward thrust of the boat to set the hook. The rod bent, and *Candide*'s first marlin was on.

Garrett had learned another Australian technique from the videotape—backing down on or otherwise following the fish, and bringing it to gaff as quickly as possible, while it was still suffering the shock of being hooked. Marlin, it seems, often make the mistake of jumping themselves into exhaustion during the first few minutes after hookup. Under such circumstances a fish can be taken without a prolonged fight, reducing stress on tackle and fisherman alike. On the Great Barrier Reef, in fact, a number of fish over 1000 pounds have been boated in a matter of minutes through use of this technique. Although not especially sporting in *The Old Man and the Sea* sense, it is a murderously efficient method. Murderous, too, on deckhands, who have suffered severed limbs in "wiring" uncooperative still-green fish.

On the other hand, we had heard that if a marlin survived those early minutes, the fisherman might be in for more than he had bargained for. There are documented accounts of experienced anglers fighting huge

---

A few hours of staring at the water in hopes of seeing signs of fish had us hallucinating at every ripple and shouting false alarms until, growing weary, we began dozing off in the heat of the famous mid-day sun...

marlin for 15 or 20 hours, and being carried beaten and exhausted from the fighting chair like unconscious boxers. A few years ago, in New Zealand's Bay of Plenty, a huge billfish battled for more than 31 hours before finally breaking away.

Our struggle was considerably less dramatic. The marlin didn't jump and didn't tear out line. It must have been gagging on the bait we had offered. Garrett reversed the engines and backed down on the fish as Caputo, not knowing what else to do, furiously took in line. The marlin seemed to sleep on. But if the fish was in a state of shock, so were we. It was close aboard in four minutes flat, but we were unprepared to deal with it. With Garrett screaming and cursing at the poor fish as well as at us, Stammers grabbed for the wire leader as London stumbled around the cluttered cockpit trying to find the flying gaff. "I know we had one when we left Florida," he wailed. The marlin waited patiently, although it was clear from Caputo's language that he was close to convulsions. At last Jack liberated the gaff from behind the cooler and, after untangling its line, stabbed at the fish with the huge hook. Needless to say, he missed, and the fish, its patience finally spent, suddenly surged under the boat. Phil had been so busy swearing that he had neglected to throw the reel into free-spool, and the result was that the line snapped on one of the propellers.

The screw-up threw us into a funk. It had been a good-sized fish—well over 200 pounds—and its escape led to the usual recriminations. Finkelstein, however, insisted on spouting profundities. "Well, that's what practice days are for," he said, smiling benignly.

"How would you like to practice swimming back to Havana?" Garrett bellowed from the bridge. We trolled for the rest of the afternoon without raising another marlin. That evening, at the bon-voyage party we held for the escaped fish, we sipped daiquiris and mojitos (rum, lemon juice and soda water) at La Bodeguita del Medio, a small bohemian grotto in the old quarter of Havana, made famous in the 'forties by such celebrities as Hemingway and Rita Hayworth, whose graffiti still adorn its walls.

On the second and final practice day we fished from noon until 6:30 P.M., which were to be actual tournament hours. *Candide* trolled her familiar zigzag along the edge of the Stream just off Morro Castle at the mouth of Havana harbor, a place where the river flows into the depths close to shore and draws big fish to feed. The tropic sun smoldered, and the heat radiating off the decks enveloped us. How, we wondered, had Hemingway been able to consume so much booze when he fished these waters on his *Pilar?* "The best beer is Hatuey," he had written, referring to the drink he most enjoyed while trolling off Havana. Perhaps we weren't Real Men after all. For had we been putting them away like Hemingway, the combination of sun and alcohol would have left us comatose in the cabin most of the day.

The northeast trades sprang up in mid-afternoon, bringing some relief. We had two strikes during the day. Another marlin hit when Caputo was in the chair, but it was smart enough to spit out the bait instantly. The second fish, unseen as it came up from below, hit when Finkelstein was nodding off during one of his turns in the chair. And when Garrett, feeling pretty cocky by now, hit the throttles, the thrust of the boat yanked a barracuda out of the water so forcefully that it shot up like a Poseidon missile.

That evening we dined at the 1830, a waterfront restaurant near the hotel. There we discovered Cabeza de Lobo Negra, a deliciously rich, dark beer similar to Guinness Stout. The maitre'd, a distinguished-looking grey-haired gentleman, chatted with us after dinner, reminiscing about the old days when "important people" frequented the restaurant. He didn't say it outright, but we could sense a wistful preference for those times, when sophisticated patrons could appreciate fine food and gracious service, and could show their appreciation with pesos. He seemed pleased, as did most Cubans we met, to see Americanos again, even if he could offer them only a poor Bulgarian wine.

The tournament began the next day at noon. The marina that morning was a frenzy of activity. Mates on all the boats were sharpening hooks, rigging baits and checking tackle. Gleaming Penn Internationals, and even fancier Fin-Nors, were in evidence as skippers, using pull-scales, adjusted reel drags to desired tensions. Not on *Candide,* however. Our tackle was more suitable for a wedding—it was both old and borrowed—and Garrett didn't have a pull scale. The chief instrument he consulted was Bob Eber's watch, and at 11:30 *Candide* joined 29 boats on their way to the starting line, where a small cannon was to be fired at noon to signal the beginning of the day's hunt for marlin. The crews had been assured by a Cuban wag that the cannon would be fired in the air and not at their boats.

The start was fouled, like most well-laid plans in Cuba, when a flare rather than a cannon was fired five minutes too early, at a time when many of the tournament's 30 boats were still on their way. When it came to confusion, *Candide* and her crew were in their element; we got away fast and stayed with the leaders all the way to the fishing grounds. We reached Cojimar, a fishing village about seven miles east of Havana, and started to troll back in a westerly direction towards Morro Castle, running the usual zigzag and probing the edge of the Stream where azure and indigo merged.

The night before, two Cuban fishermen had told Garrett that there were many large marlin in the strong current between Cojimar and Morro Castle. He was following their advice, although he had become skeptical when one of them spoke of cleaning Hemingway's boat in the old days. So many old-timers in Key West and Cuba claim to have performed this service for Hemingway that it's a wonder his *Pilar,* which is now permanently at rest on the lawn of his former villa on the outskirts of Havana, ever left its mooring.

We saw no action that day; the only excitement was listening to the radio while captains called to report hookups or fish boated. We listened with ambivalent feelings, sharing the excitement and relishing each respite from the tedium of trolling, but—since they weren't our fish—secretly hoping for breakoffs. Back at the marina that evening, the mood was festive as ten blue marlin and a few sailfish were suspended from the racks, their weights and the names of their conquistadores painted in white on their sides. Now mere grey-blue slabs of meat hanging by their tails as if they had never been alive, these once-magnificent creatures had been prowling the Stream just a few hours before.

We spent that night at the Floridita which, famous for its daiquiris, had been another haunt of Hemingway's. Looking wistfully at the marble bust of the great man at the port side of the bar, Phil wondered aloud whether it was there to honor his literary accomplishments, his fishing prowess, or his drinking feats. Caputo, Pulitzer-prizewinning newspaperman, and author of *A Rumor of War* and *Horn of Africa,* observed that if one of us could catch a good fish, he might be a match for Hemingway on all three counts and merit a matching bust on the starboard side. The bartenders didn't seem as amiable as Pedrico of *Islands in the Stream,* and whores like Honest Lil were no longer in evidence. But degenerate-looking, mysterious foreigners were draped over the bar in the frigidly air-conditioned room, staring in stony silence at the glasses in front of them while tourist groups were led in by Cubatours guides to savor the Floridita's too-sweet version of an otherwise pleasant drink.

The second day was a fishing nightmare. Black rain squalls moved down from the mountains, kicking up the water and making fishing nearly impossible. Trolling baits over a water surface buffeted by driving wind and rain was an exercise in futility. At one point during a particularly blinding downpour, Phil Caputo, in a display of courage and devotion to duty, crawled out of the cabin, shivering and weak with fever, and fell into the fighting chair so as not to miss his chance at a marlin. But all to no avail.

The weather cleared that evening, and the Cubans arranged a barbecue for the fishermen at a nearby beach. Buses took us along the coast road to the east, through a toll gate that no longer took tolls because they were considered a vulgar vestige of capitalism. Our arrival was heralded by a colorfully dressed band of musicians who played brassy Cuban music as we helped ourselves to heaping platefuls of roast suckling pig and black beans and rice, washing it down with mojitos, daiquiris and cold Hatuey beer. Entertainers from the renowned Tropicana nightclub had been recruited for the occasion, performers whose costumes looked left over from a 1941 Carmen Miranda movie. As the evening progressed and the mood became more torrid, the beautiful dancers beckoned and the bewitched fishermen joined them on the dance floor. Disco-boogying to third world solidarity songs unlikely ever to reach the record charts in the States—one especially frenzied number was creatively entitled "Africa and Cuba"—Garrett and Dick were having such a good time that we feared they might jump ship and head into the cane fields for the harvest.

The third tournament day was designated Captain's Day, signifying that any fish caught would be credited to the captain as well as the angler for the purpose of determining the winner of a "Best Captain" award. Early in the afternoon, again with Phil in the chair, a huge marlin came up and slashed at the ersatz teaser that Garrett had fashioned out of an orange-juice can. Dick yanked the teaser away and the enraged fish, turning irridescent blue in its fury, exploded from the water and devoured the bait. The line snapped from the outrigger and Garrett, by now an old pro, gunned the boat. The fish jumped clear of the water, violently thrashing its head in an effort to lose the hook, then hurtled toward the horizon in a series of greyhound leaps while line tore off the screaming reel.

The engines whined in reverse as *Candide* backed down on the streaking fish, burying her transom in a wall of water. The marlin fought spectacularly, jumping again and again with wild shakes of its head. Abandoning that tactic, it tore off line on long, powerful runs, and that failing it sounded and went deep. Taking a large fish depends primarily on the skipper's boat-handling skills—and on a considerable degree of luck. Years of experience as a clamdigger had given Garrett the necessary know-how, and he managed a number of critical maneuvers which enabled

> At one point during a particularly blinding downpour, Phil Caputo, in a display of courage and devotion to duty, crawled out of the cabin, shivering and weak with fever, and fell into the fighting chair...

Phil to hold onto the fish. When the marlin ran, Garrett pursued it, either backing down or turning and chasing it. When the fish was too deep and too close, or tried to dive directly under the boat, Garrett moved off to get more leverage on it.

Phil, meanwhile, was having the thrill of his life. By keeping the fish in the position he wanted it, he could "pull as well as lift it." Phil kept maximum pressure on the marlin, "straining rod, arms, shoulders, back and legs." Throughout the long battle, Phil told us of actually being able to "feel the marlin sensually." At one point, however, drained and exhausted, he almost gave in to the incredible strength and stamina of the fish. But Garrett compared him to an impotent Don Juan and the insult stung enough to bring him back to the battle. He had this fish where he wanted it, and he would really work it now, he told us. Breathing heavily, the powerful ex-Marine felt the fish yield. For Phil it was a moment of exhilaration. "I can feel it," he whispered, increasing his efforts, while Dick Stammers poured water on the smoking, overheated reel. Finally, after three and a half hours, the huge blue marlin was lying on its side close to the boat, spent and defeated.

Garrett got a tail-rope around the fish and began to hoist it with the gin pole, but the thick metal pole, which had a certified lifting capacity of 500 pounds, began to bend under the weight. So in the end the great fish was bound with rope and hauled aboard with the aid of the anchor line and winch, while Caputo, Stammers and Anger held it lovingly and guided it onto the deck. "You've finally done it," said Garrett to Phil. "You've brought it off." The exhausted angler stood over the captured fish, dripping perspiration.

Candide limped back to Barlovento on one engine, for during the later stages of the battle the starboard engine had overheated and Garrett had shut it down. We were greeted excitedly at the marina. Our fish weighed in at 569 pounds, and the Cubans told us that this was a new record for the largest of its species ever taken on rod and reel in Cuban waters. Immediately rumors began to circulate that a bust of Phil Caputo, considerably larger than Hemingway's, had been commissioned by the Cuban government and would shortly be unveiled at the Floridita. In all the years he fished the Stream off Havana, the largest blue marlin Hemingway himself brought aboard weighed 468 pounds. Both champagne corks and tempers exploded at the marina that night. When the dollar-a-pound prize for the largest fish failed to materialize, a brawl nearly broke out among the crews of several boats, including ours. But cooler heads prevailed, and another Cuban crisis was averted.

The last tournament day began with *Candide* listed first in all categories. But because of our engine problem there was doubt whether she would participate. Garrett dismantled the water pump but found nothing amiss. After checking to see whether a collapsed hose might be the trouble, he refitted the pump and primed it manually. Crew members from other boats came by to express their hope that we'd get out. We knew, of course, they didn't mean it.

Garrett started the engine. At first our hearts sank—there was not even a flow of water in the filter, let alone a surge. But then it came bubbling through, and the engine didn't overheat. *Candide* was cast off and cruised to the starting line. As usual, the flare was fired before all the boats were in position. But it didn't matter to us. We moved along cautiously, well under top speed, afraid that engine trouble would put us out of action at any moment. We reached the edge of the Stream just off Morro Castle, the site of the previous day's phenomenal hookup, and got the baits out.

Luck is anything but a lady, for she's blind to justice. There were three anglers aboard *Candide,* and each shared equally in hour-long sessions in the chair. Yet during the whole tournament, even on the practice days, every marlin strike occurred with Caputo in the chair. Finkelstein was the barracuda specialist, since he was in the chair for every one of the four that hit. London was the suntan expert and winner of the Jonah trophy because he didn't have a single fish on of any kind throughout the week.

Phil was in the chair this day when another huge blue, its head out of water and its bill slashing, crashed a bait from the side. The outrigger pin released as Dick screamed "knockdown!" The routine was familiar. Garrett gunned the boat ahead. As the boat surged, the line went taut and the rod bent. But this hookup was different. There was suddenly a loud bang, like a pistol shot, and the rod instantly straightened. The line had snapped. We knew the reel had suffered from the torture of the day before. When we had set the drag that morning, it had felt rough and uneven, but we couldn't repair it without spare parts. Since, to the crew of *Candide*, the word "spare" had something to do only with bowling, the reel's faulty drag and our faulty planning had cost us the opportunity for another trophy fish. It was the only strike we had that day. But later in the afternoon, as

> We were greeted
> excitedly at the marina. Our fish
> weighed in at 569 pounds, and the Cubans
> told us that this was
> a new record for the largest of
> its species ever taken on
> rod and reel in Cuban waters...

the committee boat counted down the last two minutes of the tournament, we knew we had won nonetheless.

Our Cuban sponsors organized a farewell party at the marina that evening to award trophies. The dancers from the Tropicana were back, and began performing shortly after dark. Crocodile steak was featured on the menu, and the familiar daiquiries and mojitos flowed again. As the fishermen were applauding an especially hot number, the Cuban tournament organizers mounted the stage and took their seats. Abruptly the mood changed from gaiety to solemnity. Loudspeakers blasted first the Cuban and then the American national anthems on badly scratched records while everyone stood and tried to make the subtle transformation from drunkenness to patriotism. An English-speaking master of ceremonies, whose tailor must have designed more tents than clothes, introduced our hosts, bureaucratic types he referred to as "comrade."

The MC then got down to the serious business of making the trophy presentations. Phil Caputo, of course, took both the Largest Fish and the Tournament Winner trophies, and Garrett Anger walked off the platform hugging a huge Best Captain trophy. London later dreamed that a reluctant Caputo, unwilling to be the object of the homage and adulation heaped upon him, had to be forced onto the stage by the rest of us. And that, refusing to take any credit for his achievements, he had finally been convinced to accept the awards on behalf of *Candide's* extraordinary crew rather than himself.

The following morning, as we were preparing for the return passage to Key West, a flatbed truck delivered our marlin to the boat. As if the trophies were insufficient, Phil and Garrett had decided, without consulting the others, to take the monster back to Florida as a memento, but the 13-foot-long fish was frozen stiff and too cumbersome to budge. At one point, Phil and Garrett discussed such possibilities as getting a crane to swing the fish aboard and leaving some of the crew behind, but when Bob Eber sensibly suggested that a photo of the fish might do, they seemed mollified enough by the suggestion to accept it.

But not for long. After the photo session, Phil and Garrett withdrew to confer with one another. Then Garrett jumped aboard *Candide,* returning moments later with a saw in his hand. He and Phil leapt on the truck, and to everyone's amazement they proceeded to saw through the frozen corpse. It looked almost like some primitive rite, and we half expected them to devour the severed parts. But instead of eating them, they hauled the crescent-shaped tail and enormous head to the boat. As we limped homeward, again on one engine, we tried to ignore the huge eye that stared unforgivingly from the great head lying in the cockpit.

Later, Phil would explain that Garrett had offered him his "captain's discount"—he had offered to forego his captain's commission—if the fish were mounted. Never one to pass up a good offer, Phil paid a mere $2000 to enshrine the marlin and immortalize his achievement. If in life the mighty fish had ruled the Gulf Stream, its plastic likeness would now dominate Phil's house, occupying a place of honor on one wall of his library where a number of lesser trophies had been mounted.

Following a triumphant return to Key West, at a hastily arranged press conference, the "heroes of Barlovento" were asked by an impertinent reporter why it had been necessary to kill the marlin. In an unusual display of physical coordination, Finkelstein leapt to his feet and was about to confess that the crew of *Candide* also had doubts about what they had done. But a calm Phil Caputo cut him off with a wave of his hand. He reflected for a moment, collecting his thoughts. Then, acting as though he were spokesman for all of us, he phrased an eloquent reply: "I don't want to sound brutal, but even if releases had been counted in the tournament, I wouldn't have released that marlin. When you get into a contest like that, the death of the fish becomes emotionally necessary. It's like killing the bull in a bullfight...People may think it's unfair, but it's a dishonor to the fish *not* to kill it. They can call me a blood-luster, but that's what I feel. You go out for the nobility of the contest. And you haven't completed the circuit until it's yours—until you've killed it."

This adventure ends not in Cuba, nor even in Key West. For on the following day Finkelstein and Anger drove to Miami International Airport and boarded a flight to New York. As they sat there reliving the excitement of the trip, Garrett suddenly realized that he'd left his trophy in the waiting room. Finkelstein asked the crew to hold the flight, and Garrett raced off the plane, picked up his trophy, and returned. Fame is a fleeting commodity—what means so much to some means less than nothing to others. Garrett's Best Captain trophy—a handsome silver cup set on a long spindle—had been mistaken for an ashtray. Waiting passengers had left its bottom littered with ashes, stubbed cigarettes and a cigar butt or two. Sic transit gloria marlin.

> He and Phil leapt on the truck, and to everyone's amazement they proceeded to saw through the frozen corpse. It looked almost like some primitive rite, and we half expected them to devour the severed parts...

DER MINI-ZWÖLFER

A SMALL BOAT BEGINS A LONG JOURNEY

TEXT AND PHOTOGRAPHS BY PETER NEUMANN

The winds were quiet at Cowes. It was August 7, 1981—a day when the cream of the world's ocean racing fraternity should have been mixing it up on the race course in that biennial challenge, the Admiral's Cup. Not a whisper of wind was to be had, not for love, not for money. The second inshore race that morning had first been postponed and then canceled for the day. The international competitors—wound as tight that morning as they ever are—were now ashore in crowded Cowes, looking for action in desultory fashion. □ Near noon, a small 12′ scale model of an America's cup 12 Meter took to the water, and a lone sailor, who literally filled her cockpit, sailed her around the marina, passing a world's worth of ocean-racing yachts from nearly 20 countries and their very bored crews. The response to this little keel boat, with its unusual foot-pedal steering and racecar-like cockpit, was out of proportion to its size. A crowd of suddenly very interested racers queued up to sail this mini 12, aptly named *Illusion*.

Even before the appearance of the grand *Illusion*, there was no boredom on the German Admiral's Cup yacht *Dusselboot*. There wasn't time for it with a mast to be repaired—a casualty of the Channel Race. At the sight of the little *Illusion*, tacking and gybing on the opaque waters of the River Medina, one of the crew muttered, "I could get into that." His remark, however, was lost in the still air, what with the task at hand.

Later that night in Cowes, the *Dusselboot* crew sat relaxing under a large chestnut tree in the garden they "owned" for the fortnight of Cowes. They shared a bottle of wine and their thoughts. The theme of this meandering discussion was the next sailing project. They discussed the possibility of campaigning a maxi ocean racer. That, however, was rejected because none of them was particularly keen on long ocean races. They were most at home, it was agreed, racing 'round the buoys.

The conversation wandered to the America's Cup, but such an idea was rejected when the cost of mounting such a campaign began to be estimated. Without infinitely deep pockets, the group discussed the difficulties of finding sponsorship and large-scale financing. The biggest problem, they reasoned, was in educating potential sponsors and the German public about the America's Cup and how it is sailed:

> A boat like that might be the perfect first step with which to begin a long journey to the America's Cup.

match racing. Match racing, although common in America in other such competitions as the Congressional Cup, the Prince of Wales Cup, and the Richardson Cup, is not so familiar in European sailing circles.

Someone remembered *Illusion*, that miniature "12 Meter" that had caught the waterfront's fancy earlier in the day. It occurred to him that a boat like that might be the perfect first step with which to begin a long journey to the America's Cup. What if, it was posed, we start a one-design class of these scaled-down one-man 12 meters? That then might:

☐ Generate a wealth of media attention. The publicity could prove attractive to sponsors. Such publicity might also favorably influence the reaction to such sponsorship by the official sailing associations, which traditionally have been unenthusiastic about corporate-sponsored yachts and sponsored yachting.

☐ Allow sponsors to test the waters, so to speak, by funding a mini 12 in competitions around Germany. If this association proved successful, sponsors might be inclined to invest in a full-size twelve for an America's Cup campaign.

☐ Provide an opportunity for the class of mini 12 Meters to turn into an end in itself, particularly if the characteristics of the boat were suitable to German sailors and German waters. Germany is a country with a short coastline, but one blessed with numerous lakes, many of them quite shallow. Thus the boat must be of light draft, as well as capable of riding on the top of an automobile and manageable by less than a rugby team in launching or removing it from the water. The boat must also feature high-performance—in the manner of a true 12 Meter—which is particularly important to the performance-oriented German sailor.

With these thoughts in mind, Rolf Vrolijk and Fiedje Judel, both yacht designers and members of the newly chartered "12er-Syndikat," turned to the drawing table. That autumn they produced the lines of a one-design boat they called the Mini-Zwölfer. They put a lot of thought into the boat and came up with something that looked like a full-sized America's Cup yacht.

Judel's comments cast quite a bit of light onto the problems of scaling down a big yacht: "We had to produce a boat that would look like the original, perform like the original, but only be

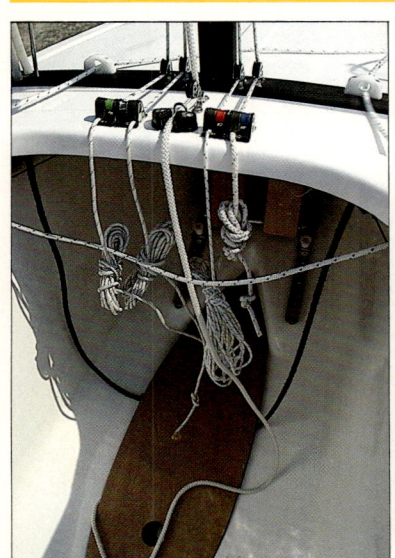

Far left, halyards and sundry sail-control lines lead to the cockpit, and the tiny "12s" are steered with foot pedals to keep hands free. Left, a sailor is weighed so that sailing weights are kept equal. The boats ship lead ballast to accomplish this end. Right, *Fielmann* takes to the water. On the opposite page, the boats float quite high until the sailor and ballast are added.

sailed by one person—not at all like the original. The boat had to be as small as possible, but nevertheless it had to offer the necessary safety.

"Complications were to be expected in drawing the underwater shape. We designed the boat around the body of an average-size sailor, thus necessitating that the underwater midships section have the appearance of an expectant mother, with full U-shaped lines. We calculated a total displacement of 220 kilograms (484 pounds) of which 80 kilograms were lead ballast. After the prototype's sail trials, keel weight was increased to 90 kilos for better stability in heavier winds.

"The safety of a small boat like this was of supreme importance. We incorporated a second skin to keep the boat and helmsman afloat should the boat swamp. The results of Rolf's and my thinking can be seen: the mini 12 is a singlehanded, pedal-steered, high-performance yacht with every conceivable sail-trim option on the smallest possible platform. It is a boat supporting 5.1 square meters of sail—that is without counting a 2.8-square-meter spinnaker. The hull is 3 meters (10′) long, 78 cm (2′7″) at the beam, and has a draft of 70 cm. The yacht is made of fiberglass with Firet-Vlies (a sort of velvetlike cloth) for the core material to keep the weight of the hull down.

"The problems of the rig were solved, amusingly enough, by adapting a shortened (aluminum) sailboard mast. We added double spreaders to give the rig a 12-Meter appearance and fitted a groove in it for the luff of the mainsail. To simplify transportation and to insure fast stepping and unstepping, the mast is secured to the deck with only two bolts. The stays are made of 2.5-mm rod rigging, and backstay is, of course, adjustable. All sheets and halyards are led to the cockpit where they are in easy reach of the helmsman."

On a late-autumn day, the seven members of the 12er-Syndikat displayed what they had wrought at a press conference at the Norddeutscher Regatta Verein (NRV)—the principal ocean-racing club in Germany. The syndicate announced a list of sponsors and exhibited the first production version of the mini 12 to a public which seemed astounded. The controversial idea of corporate sponsorship was openly discussed, as was the possibility of Germany removing that so-called "immovable mug," the America's Cup, from the New York Yacht Club.

In January, 1982, the new 12-Meter syndicate hosted its own exhibit at Dusseldorf—one of Europe's largest boat shows. This show's focal point is a huge pool with a "wind machine"—a large fan. In the pool, sailing demonstrations are possible, and there the Mini-Zwölfers made their spectacular debut, with an impressive display of tacking, gybing, and quick maneuvering. After the exhibition closed, the pleasantly surprised syndicate members claimed the sale of boats to five countries. Perhaps the most prominent purchaser was Bruno Troublé, helmsman of *France III* in the America's Cup.

The German effort to challenge for the America's Cup gathered further momentum in the spring as the first of ten match-racing regattas was held in Hamburg. There were ten sponsored yachts involved in the competition. Name-brand sailors from the world of dinghy and ocean racing were invited to race the boats, and the participation of sponsors—both on and off the race course—was encouraged.

Before the competition, racers were weighed

> There the Mini-Zwölfers made their spectacular debut, with an impressive display of tacking, gybing and quick maneuvering.

so as to keep all-up weights equal. Spectators seemed to enjoy this weighing-in ceremony. The "underfed" were required to ship ballast in the form of lead blocks with handles for easy toting. A commentator kept the crowd apprised of the finer points of match racing—for example, why *Porsche* was tacking to windward of *Helly Hanson*. Courses were kept short—the windward leg was 150 meters—and oriented close to shore for the benefit of spectators. The format adopted for 12er racing is a single-elimination contest. The last man "standing" gets weighed at the end, although this time his weight is balanced by some other happily disposable and sharable product of a sponsor, such as beer. The last event of the competition is a fleet race. To the victor of this finale goes "the green band of sympathy," a bronze sculpture provided by Dresdner, one of Germany's largest banks.

The future of the mini 12s seems rosy. More than 70 boats have been built, and there are orders for another hundred from all over Europe and from Japan. This past autumn, the minis held their first European championship.

The 12er-Syndikat has not lost sight of its first priority: an America's Cup entry for 1986. The mini 12s seem to have been an excellent first step for Germany's first challenge to the America's Cup. To this end, the syndicate has been reorganized into three management efforts: (1) marketing, (2) financial coordination, and (3) technical coordination and crew organization.

There is one more stop along the road before a full-size 12 is tackled. That is a Six Meter—already tank-tested—which will sail in 1983. Later in the year, with the cooperation of sponsors and German universities, the lines for one or two full-size 12s will be produced. Assisting in this huge technical undertaking are a sophisticated computer analysis and extensive data bank. The syndicate expects to see its first two 12s sailing in the summer of 1984. That will give the effort plenty of time for further development, if necessary.

In May of 1985, if all goes according to plan, Newport will welcome a new debutante to the party, the snow-white "Made in Germany," as her name will be. It is a long road, perhaps—from a miniature 12 Meter seen on a breathless day in Cowes in 1981 to the America's Cup in 1986—but, as the saying goes, "The journey of a thousand miles must begin with a single step."

Acres of spinnaker cloth—2.8 square meters to be precise—drive der Mini-Zwölfers downwind at hull speed. According to our calculations, hull speed for this 10 feet of yacht is about four knots. On the opposite page, *Storage Technology* sits on the wind of *Helly Hanson*, while spectators enjoy the show. Without the heads, the illusion would be perfect.

"While traveling on business I came upon your magazine in the lounge of the St. Francis Yacht Club. I was overwhelmed by the artistry of your publication. I have never seen such striking photography and such compelling layouts. Your articles are equally first-rate. I was literally unable to put it down, and ended up taking it with me when I left—which may make me <u>persona non grata</u> at this club in the future."

Unsolicited testimonial
from a NAUTICAL QUARTERLY
subscriber/sailor

NAUTICAL QUARTERLY

WORTH STEALING FOR.

BUT WHY RISK IT?

 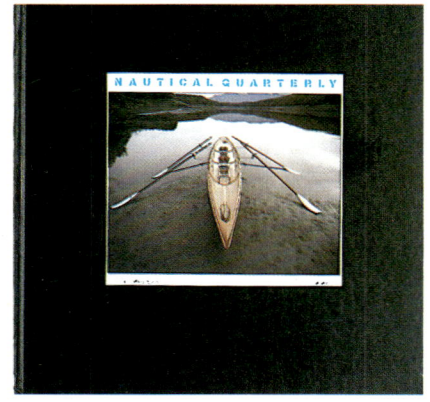 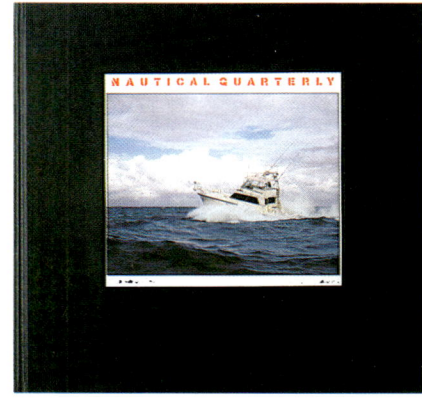 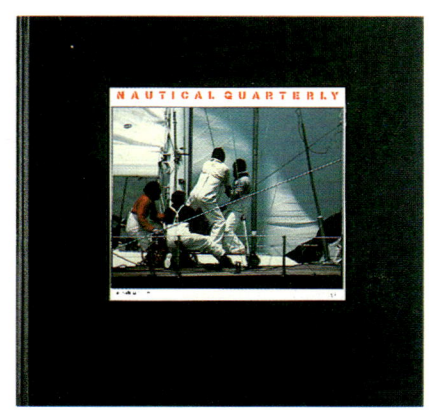

For subscriptions or gifts, use the attached order form or write us:
NAUTICAL QUARTERLY, 373 Park Ave. South, New York, NY 10016 U.S.A.

NAUTICAL QUARTERLY

SHANNON 50 — A SURVEY BY FRASER AND JEAN FRASER-HARRIS

The Shannon story has potential as a modern-day version of "David and Goliath." Walter Schulz, owner and working President of the company, is good casting for the role of David, who had the ingenuity to employ a simple slingshot against the armor of a giant.

The unusual feature of Shannon Yachts, apart from their logo which Jean describes as a 'seagoing twig,' is that their pedigree is due almost entirely to the character of this one man who is himself designer, engineer and company director. This is by no means to say that Walter Schulz alone is responsible for the quality these yachts display. It is to say that his practical management skill, resting as it does upon a philosophy of trust and consequential loyalty among company personnel from top to bottom, produces a common focus and devotion to quality that is a treat to observe.

Walter Schulz, now in his thirties, grew up in and around City Island and worked his way through college, learning as a youngster the basics of all the yachtbuilding trades. His curiosity and enthusiasm assured his welcome among the old timers in the famous yards where he served a thorough apprenticeship.

At 17 he invested in an old truck and, using it as a mobile workshop, did everything from rebuilding engines during the long winter months to cabinetry and brightwork in spring and summer.

Having won a degree in Fine Arts he became, in his words, "a suit man," joining the rat race in the advertising business, first illustrating and then copywriting. He was bored stiff, even though he still indulged his sailoring instinct by the purchase of old boats to dish up for re-sale. Eventually he and his young wife came to a decision that there was more to life than money. They sold their house, moved aboard a 30-footer Walter had just completed and took off.

This didn't work either. Doing nothing would suit Walter Schulz as well as water a cat. Watching a yacht-yard crew at work ashore he decided that, really, that was where he belonged. Shortly thereafter, employed as a yard manager, he found himself doing a good deal of commissioning and warranty work for new domestic boats and imports. What he saw, and compared with the standards of his boyhood training, triggered his career. He knew that he could do better. David took aim at Goliath.

Twenty years later the old Dodge truck

still decorates his garage, and the Shannon Boat Company personnel celebrate its birthday annually.

This is a survey of the Shannon 50, not the life history of Walter Schulz, but without question the yacht reflects the ideas and ideals of this man. To relate the story of one is to take the measure of the other.

What is the Shannon objective? Returning to Walter: his hero was Henry Hinckley, Sr. When fiberglass began to replace wood, Hinckley saw in the material not the opportunity to adopt production-line techniques, reduce costs and produce volume at the expense of individuality and quality, but rather to adapt the new material to the building of more efficient and even higher-quality yachts than could be built of wood. To match the old man's standards became Walter's ambition.

The Shannon workshops are in Bristol because history, Schulz' other passion, had established Rhode Island as a center of fine boatbuilding. The old Herreshoff plant had been there since the last century. Clint and Everett Pearson, founding fathers of fiberglass, were there. Portuguese immigration had brought both skill and a strong work ethic in recent decades to the area's yachtbuilding industry. This mixture of the Fine-Arts major's sense of tradition with the practical approach of an experienced sailor and skilled craftsman delineate the characteristics of the vessel we are appraising. All Shannons—and there are only four models now in production—the 28′, 38′, Pilot 38′, and 50′—have the same design philosophy: no concession is made to any rating rule or "Madison Avenue" sales criteria. These boats are described by the old-fashioned term "sailing auxiliaries," which is exactly what they are—oceangoing cruising yachts designed to go fast under sail, provide comfortable liveaboard accommodations with adequate space for stowage of gear and provisions, carry ample tankage for long-range cruising, and incorporate efficient and accessible engineering systems. Because they are designed by a sailor they are also seamanlike in appearance; they are good-looking in the traditional sense, and built to last. Schulz believes there will always be a market for quality, and we agree with him. Those who get hooked by the sea and are also wealthy want the best. They will look for a boat big enough to cruise with their friends, maybe carry a professional skipper to look after maintenance and ease the workload, yet not be so large that she cannot be handled comfortably by two people.

Having designed the vessel to meet the cruising sailor's criteria, the attainment of maximum quality control is achieved by following three salient management principles: first, minimize subcontracting with its consequential loss of quality control; secondly, keep your work force small enough to permit personal contact with a highly skilled and well-motivated team; and, thirdly, limit your annual production to what can be competently handled by this team in the available man-hours.

Shannon's office space is small and crowded—no shag carpet and fancy furniture—but the shops are nicely laid out. The president's desk is a drawing board! Shannon has its own design and engineering facility. Walter Schulz and prototype engineer John Procter pioneer systems such as the hydraulic bow thrusters installed in the 50—an "in-house" development; spars are purchased as bare extrusions and finished in the rigging shop, and wood is bought as raw timber to insure well-seasoned lumber.

Before tackling construction details of the 50, a final comment on the work force. To encourage maximum understanding of their jobs, cross-training courses are run during the winter months. Thus, every employee gains a basic knowledge of the other trades involved in building one of these boats, a thing that furthers understanding and cooperation overall. In the summer, sail training is run for those interested, and all are expected to go aboard for experience afloat. Successful graduates of the sailing courses are rewarded with delivery trips, or are lent to owners to assist on passages. Shannon also writes the name of every man who works on a boat on the bottom of a drawer in the main cabin. It is not, therefore, surprising that we found considerable esprit de corps in evidence on the shop floors.

The molding shop has good ventilation, and electric heating coils built into the concrete floor sustain an even room temperature for controlled curing during the winter months. In this shop, under the direction of Steve Butterworth assisted by such highly skilled technicians as David Saraiva and Raphael Pinheiro, who learned his trade back in 1961 under Clint Pearson's able guidance, hulls are laid up in one piece in fiberglass molds. Shannon prefers this practice to the split-mold technique wherein two halves of a hull are subsequently joined together; the builder believes (particularly with integral ballast) that the result is stronger and justifies the extra labor involved. The mold itself, however, is split for ease of "breakout" when the hull layup has cured.

The integral ballast, which consists of five interlocking lead castings surrounding the centerboard trunk, is held in place with "casting resin," built up slowly to avoid heat in curing, finally forming a solid inside the 2″ laminate at the base of the keel. The total ballast weight is 15,500 pounds, of which some 500 pounds are in ingots glassed to the hull in various places to achieve final trim after all optional equipment is installed.

The hull is a solid 1″ laminate up to the waterline or turn of the bilge, from which point up to the sheer it is Airex-cored. The reasoning is sound: the hull, being solid on the bottom but cored on the topsides, has a weight distribution that lowers the center of gravity and thus improves the sailing performance. In addition, the cored topsides provide good acoustic and thermal insulation. The design includes a solid and effective rubrail.

Hull layup takes nine days, the topside laminate being ⅜″ glass, ¾″ Airex and 5⁄16″ internal glass, to a total of over 1″. All fiberglass work is done by hand. To insure consistent quality of resin, every drum of each batch is checked daily for "kick-off" time, with catalyst adjustments made to compensate for temperature and humidity

One of two Shannon 50 interior plans, this one places a U-shaped galley amidships to starboard, and the owner's cabin is aft. In an alternate plan, the large owner's stateroom fits amidship and the galley aft.

LOA: 50′11″
LWL: 42′9″
Beam: 14′3″
Draft: 7′0″ (keel version) 5′8″ (centerboard version—board up) 9′9″ (centerboard version—board down)
Sail Area: 1227 sq. ft. (ketch), 1317 sq. ft. (staysail schooner), 1326 sq. ft. (foresail schooner)
Ballast: 15,500 pounds
Displacement: 39,000 pounds
Fuel: 150 gallons
Water: 300 gallons
Power: Perkins Engine Co. 85-hp diesel
Spars: aluminum
Hull: hand-layup fiberglass with Airex-core topsides
Designer: Walter Schulz
Builder: Shannon Boat Co., 19 Broad Common Rd., Bristol, R.I. 02809

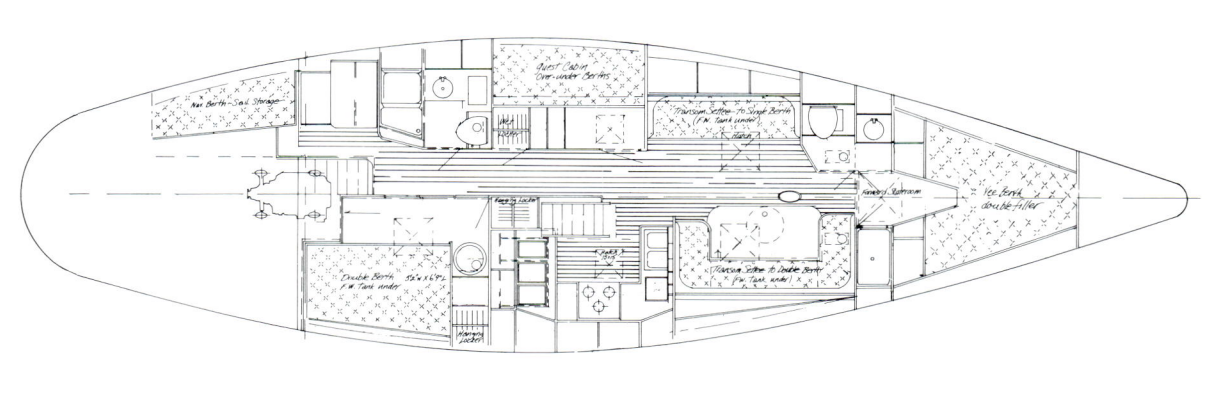

variations.

The deck/coachroof laminate uses Kontacore—about 2" squares of end-grain balsa with a cloth backing forming sheets easily cut to selected shapes. Plywood reinforces all vulnerable points where the laminate will be penetrated by fittings. Unidirectional "S" glass strengthens the area of attachment for the chainplates as well as other particular stress points. The interior of the hull is coated with fire-retardant resin. We were impressed by the meticulous care with which six young men were working on the deck molding, where there was no skimping on resin. However, having seen during my survey work so many problems created by moisture penetration of balsa cores, I would recommend the additional step of actually dipping the Kontacore sheets in a tray of resin before their introduction to the lay-up, to secure resin penetration between the blocks.

The hull/deck joint is on an 8" internal flange. A ¾" ash plank, glassed in under the flange along the length of the sheer, supplies additional strength and compression "bite" for the through bolts. The deck molding is laid on a base of epoxy putty which remains soft, providing a complete waterproof seal but some flexibility to the joint. The bolting schedule is ⅜" stainless on 8" centers to secure the deck, with similar ⅜" stainless bolts securing the teak toe rail on alternate 8" centers. Finally, the genoa track, which covers the middle 70% of the sheer, is also through-bolted with ⅜" stainless. Thus, 70% of the joint on each side is bolted at 2" centers, the remaining 30% at 4" centers, altogether a strong and rigid job of construction engineering.

The surface finish is a high-grade deck tread, with both the texture and the color molded in. This, in our opinion, is the wiser choice over teak which, while an undeniable status symbol, is hot on the feet in the tropics. Cruising types, unlike racing men, are wont to go barefoot. In the long run, teak decks require maintenance, re-caulking and much scrubbing or preservation by oiling. Neglect of any of these gives rise to problems. Shannon's deck tread is, in our opinion, a shade too dark. Much experiment in the tropics leads me to suggest a slightly lighter shade of the same color to achieve the ideal compromise between "hot foot" and "cold stare."

On the subject of heat and color, "owners have a choice of any hull color as long as it's white." Dictatorial? Maybe—but very smart. Colored gelcoat of any age is a menace. Fading is inevitable, as is difficulty of matching in repair. Chemically, pigments may also degrade the quality of the gelcoat.

Before the decks are married to the hull, interior bulkheading is completed, the engine bed is molded in, and tanks and engine are set in place. Bulkheads and chainplate knees are 1" with plywood cores and polyester half rounds to insure good curvature of the heavy glass bonding, which also incorporates "mare's tails" of continuous strands of glass reinforcement at 8" centers, bonded to the hull to "lock" the bulkheads in place. Chainplates are 2" x ½" stainless, each with six ½" stainless bolts. The engine bearers are solid ash blocks carved to the curvature of the hull, with similar solid ash cross floors, the whole having a ¾" glass and resin covering and incorporating a built-in drip tray.

Five stainless-steel tanks give a total water capacity of 300 gallons. Two 75-gallon fuel tanks are of 5052 military spec. aluminum/magnesium alloy. All are removable to permit long-term maintenance. Freshwater plumbing is all copper with flared fittings. Heat loss on long pipe runs is eliminated by employing two standard 12-gallon water heaters, one for each shower space.

Before tackling the engineering, a word about the joinery. Here, quality and pride of workmanship are evident. Carpenters Ken Bliss and Knute Berg, a survivor of the last Herreshoff work force, echo Walter's conviction that in joinery work built to last, solid timber surpasses all forms of lamination. This, in certain applications, is a matter of opinion, for modern cold-molded laminations which we have seen in other vessels have been very impressive. In any case, the solid door frames, oak joinery and solid teak and holly (or basswood) soles built into these yachts are of unquestionable beauty and stamina.

No nail will be found in a Shannon. Glue and screw are mandatory. An interesting concession to "mass production" is that almost all drawers in the three yachts (28', 38' and 50') are set up to a standard design which permits their production in quantity, but all have half-cut rabbet joints and handsome recessed brass handles.

On the engineering side, Shannon's mechanics, electricians, and plumbers are ably directed by Kevin Waters under the guidance of production manager Mark Perry. The 50's main engine is a Perkins 4-236 diesel rated for 85 hp. Since detailed specifications are available from the builder, we will confine comment here to unusual features. Believing hydraulics to be more compatible with salt water for certain applications than is electricity, the engine's front end is modified to drive a heavy hydraulic pump which supplies power for the bow thrusters, windlass and centerboard. On the boat we sea-trialed, a 4.4-kw Westerbeke diesel generator was also installed. This is a customer option, and Hull No. 8 will carry a 7.7-kw generator. In addition, Shannon is developing a hydraulically driven generator which will run off an engine-driven pump. Despite this availability of hydraulic power, Walter Schulz does not believe in power-driven hydraulic backstays and boom vangs for this vessel, regarding such devices as unnecessarily complex for a cruising vessel. Navtec hydraulic backstay tensioners are fitted, but are manually operated.

The centerboard hoist is a wire winch with manual secondary. The pendant is so run that, in the event of the board striking bottom, it will lift, but the wire will not foul. To prevent board movement in the well, heavy and very hard rubber "wipers," inserts of about ⅝" thickness, are fitted into slots on the board. These are experimental, being intended both to prevent glass-to-glass contact between board and well and also to clean marine growth off the interior of the well when the board is operated. A great idea; Walter has his fingers crossed that the wipers will conquer a young barnacle. Given a few weeks to grow between board operations, the barnacle has my money, I fear. The owner's manual will have to specify frequent operation.

Full marks for the bow thrusters. They work, too, even though still in the Mk. I and Mk. II stages, with further modifications in the offing. It is difficult to achieve a hull form that is both highly maneuverable and directionally stable. Since a cruising yacht's No. 1 priority should be directional stability without necessity for constant attention to the wheel (which most competitive racers *do* require), the Shannon 50 is designed to be and *is* beautifully "steady on course." But she doesn't like steering astern and is, because of her relatively long keel, a bit sluggish turning at rest. The bow thrusters restore the Shannon 50's at-rest and astern mobility so that you have the best of both worlds.

A forced-air system runs the length of the accommodation both port and starboard. Air conditioning ducts are also installed to permit retrofit if required. The omission of one of these vents in the forward shower compartment is to be remedied. The placing of the forward head and shower in two separate enclosed spaces, each with a wash basin, is smart as it virtually doubles rush-hour capacity.

This is a good time to bring up consideration of interior design and company philosophy regarding owner's options. The latter is summed up nicely by Walter Schulz. "Our reputation is only as good as the last boat built," he says. What he means is that while Shannon will go a long way towards satisfying individual requirements, the company will not deviate from what they consider to be common sense, sound seamanship or good engineering practice. For example, complex electronic equipment and efficient navigation stations to customer's choice are engineered by Mike Drywa, "the 747 man," with circuitry and distribution panels built in-house to aircraft standards.

The interior of the yacht we inspected was good taste personified, but as taste is so obviously subjective we define it in this instance as the subtle combination of simplicity of line, quality of material, and efficiency of space utilization. The light oak and teak trim create a cheerful and unpretentious interior. Ventilation, as will have been gathered, is outstanding.

Galley design is conventional "U" shape, with cooking by a well-installed propane system (the tanks require individual securing devices or straps in their otherwise very satisfactory locker), and stowage space is ample, as is the capacity of the large freezer/refrigerator—a Grunert Versamatic system with generous insulation. There is even a folding step to help the short cook dive down into its recesses! A bar cabinet door swings out with a drop leaf so that cook and bar man/maid do not compete for space during the activities of the cocktail hour. (Do we now flirt with a "Barperson"? Oh Lord!)

The division of accommodation and the availability of two companionways, both fairly steep but with good handrails, give complete privacy to the owner's cabin when required. By closing sliding doors to starboard, the double berth can be isolated from the corridor and nav. station. The forward head has two doors which, again, increase privacy if the saloon is in use as a sleeping area. An upper and lower twin-berthed guest cabin is to port, enabling the yacht to cruise three couples and still accommodate a professional skipper forward. Access to the deck through the forehatch avoids disturbing guests.

On the subject of access: engine servicing is easily performed by removal of small strategically placed panels. Removal of the

> The light oak and teak trim create a cheerful and unpretentious interior. Ventilation, as will have been gathered, is outstanding.

whole front panel and entry to the after end through a cockpit engineroom hatch permit complete access for periodic inspection or maintenance.

Finally to a finished vessel. Each boat is launched, commissioned, and seatrialed by Shannon with an intensive owner orientation, including docking drills. A tradition of the company is that every vessel is christened personally with blackberry brandy by Walter Schulz. A detailed description of the deck layout would take undue space; suffice to note 6 hatches, 2 companionways and 7 large dorade ventilators. The foredeck is fairly short, but clear, the hydraulic windlass being mounted on a vast teak anchor platform where either cable can be handled satisfactorily. The teak does need protective stainless plates along the run of the chain leads. Dinghy chocks are fitted to port of the midship hatch, and there is neat stowage for the liferaft to port between the fore and after coachroofs.

Cockpit design is excellent. Seat coamings are well sloped. A nice touch is teak blocks to take the sole grating at seat level to create a lounging area which does not interfere with the helmsman. Instrumentation on the after ends of the seat moldings, both port and starboard in the helmsman's section of the cockpit, is in sight and accessible rather than being hidden behind people trying to get comfortable. A cockpit icebox cooler, hot and cold shower, and no fewer than three compasses (main 6" on the binnacle and two wing steering or bearing compasses) display the excellent approach to "everything the cruising man requires—to hand," which this yacht incorporates.

As always, we ask the reader to make allowance for opinions on the performance of a yacht which must be based upon a two- or three-hour sailing trial; obviously, we cannot take every candidate for examination across an ocean. Fortunately we had good wind, 15 gusting 20, when we sailed the Shannon 50. Aboard with us were vice president Bill Ramos and Paul Dubuc. Howard Rotblat-Walker, owner-liaison officer, who had ably and unobtrusively assisted us in the morning's explorations, was obliged to return to his desk. Bill, in Shannon tradition, handles sales and sails with equal expertise. With an Azorean Portuguese boatbuilder's background, he is also skilled in the glass shop where he helped lay up the first boat in 1975. Meanwhile, with Shannon's help, he has also put himself through law school. Paul, commissioning foreman who checks out all new owners as well as new boats, has been around almost as long, starting with Shannon when he was 16. He has considerable technical knowledge and practical ability at his command.

We carried full working sail, Yankee on Hood roller furling headstay, boomed staysail, main and mizzen. This rig provides three advantages: small individual sail areas for easy handling, minimum sheet work when tacking, (only the Yankee is tended on very adequate self-tailing winches) and a rig that can be reduced "in balance." The yacht immediately creates a good impression. With all sail set in very short order we paid off and took off. Heeling to some 12-15°, she settled down and just "went"—balance excellent, hands off.

The mainsail is cut fairly full as it should be for cruising; tack angle is between 85° and 100° with plenty of power to windward. The centerboard when lowered can be felt to bite and the wake angle straightens out, but the boat goes to windward quite satisfactorily with the board retracted. She reaches like a train and, with "wing and wing" and board up, holds speed well off the wind. "Lazy jacks," which I see have now been reinvented as "Sail Catcher" by Safe Sailing Systems, assist mainsail furling. Performance under power is quiet and efficient. Maneuvering with bow thruster assist is a snap.

We believe this vessel is a first-class, no-compromise, "state of the art" cruising yacht. It is expensive but, in our opinion, justifies its price. A Shannon yacht is bought from Shannon Boat Company. There are no agents. No new models appear every year. The boats are built to last. Contact is maintained with all owners. There have been more than 530 modifications and improvements to the 38' in the seven years since the second came out of the mold, but it is still basically the same yacht; it has stood the test of time. Four of the owners of the first six Shannon 50s are former owners of 38s, a fact that says more for the reputation of this company than any favorable comments this survey may contain.

We would recommend a securing device for the heavy, wide-opening cockpit locker lids which provide excellent access to plentiful stowage space; some rearrangement to permit access to batteries for check without removal of gear in the port locker, and external hasps for the lockers and gas-tank stowage. These, however, are small points when compared to the overall achievement of such a high standard of quality in a cruising yacht, which we deem the Shannon 50 to represent.

Many points which we have not covered are well-detailed in thorough and accurate specifications available from the builder. In conclusion, it may be relevant that this is the first company involved in these surveys which not only welcomes visits to their shop by qualified surveyors, but encourages customers to employ a qualified surveyor during construction.

These three details of the Shannon 50—amidships galley, navigator's station, and main cabin looking aft past the 50's two steep companionway ladders—show her to be a cruising vessel blessed with roomy, businesslike spaces. They also show the excellent fit and finish of joinerwork in oak and teak, and cabin soles of traditional teak splined with holly or basswood.

One of the advantages of building boats in Bristol, Rhode Island, is the quantity and quality of boat-carpentry talent in the area, a legacy of the Herreshoff Manufacturing Company, which flourished there until a generation ago, and in more recent decades a legacy from Portugal. Portuguese, Azorean and Cape Verdean immigrants have brought Bristol a strong work ethic and an old-world pride in perfect workmanship in wood.

NAUTICAT 52 —A SURVEY BY FRASER AND JEAN FRASER-HARRIS

Referred to in the Nauticat brochure as "probably the most luxurious motorsailer in modern production," this yacht might be equally well designated as a "pilothouse ketch." Before launching into our survey report, a word about the terms "motorsailer" and "pilothouse." Both have certain connotations that are not always reflected in a particular vessel. A motorsailer, for instance, in the minds of many, implies a hefty motorboat which also has some sail area, a vessel comfortable when "motorsailing" but slow under sail and a roller under power. More accurate description is achieved by percentage reference to ability under sail or power. A true motorsailer is a 50/50. It is half power and half sail. Put some sail on a diesel cruiser hull such as the Fisher or Banjer and it might be regarded as 30/70—thirty percent sail, seventy percent power. Applying the same principle to the Nauticat 52 we come up with a figure of 80/20—eighty percent sail, twenty percent power, in the case of the single-engined version. For the twin-engine version (an owner option), 70/30 would seem accurate.

Use of the term "pilothouse" should be quite specific. It is an enclosed space from which a vessel may be piloted (meaning both directed and navigated) during inclement weather or at night. It is *not* simply a roof over a cockpit or a wheel and controls in the saloon or galley. It is important to bear this in mind when assessing the merits of any motorsailer or pilothouse yacht. Since the pilothouse will be used for control during doubtful weather and at night, its purpose must not be in conflict with cooking, eating, etc., for which light is required. The "on watch" will be distracted, the "off watch" inhibited.

We think Nauticat's name would benefit from change, especially in the United States, due to its erroneous connotations in nautical language. Despite this, Siltala Yachts Oy, the builder, maintains a very honorable reputation as a Finnish boatbuilding yard near the port city of Turku, at the entrance to the Gulf of Bosnia, some 300 miles south of Jacobstad/Pietarsaari where their friends at Nautor build the Swans. Indeed the Nauticat 52 has Nautor connections, albeit somewhat remote. Maybe if they were just to drop the "at" from "cat," thus becoming "Nautic," it would help.

The company, under the direction of Pentti Siltala, began life in the early sixties producing fiberglass dinghies and small fishing vessels to local designs. In 1966, a small fiberglass motorsailer was built. The popularity of this very efficient little cruising yacht spread rapidly. By 1968, modified to become the Nauticat 33, this prototype established full production in a factory which remains to this day under the total control of the Siltala family.

Wisely, in our opinion, Siltala Yachts has remained faithful to its specialization, the building of efficient motorsailers or pilothouse types. Unfortunately, it has not been possible to visit the factory (or see the boat out of the water), a point which should be borne in mind when reading this report. However, we have managed to spend some time on two very different versions of the Nauticat 52.

To trace its lineage one must look at development of Nauticat models. These number, to date, only four: the original 33′, a 38′, a 44′ and the 52′. Following upon international acceptance of the 33 as a high-quality motorsailer somewhere in the 60/40 sail-to-power ratio, came the 44, a considerably larger yacht of similar characteristics. Molds for the 38-footer were purchased from a Danish company and much modified, going into production as a yacht emphasizing greater sailing potential, raising the ratio to perhaps 70/30.

Pentti Siltala appears to be a man who does not look the other way in the face of opportunity. Nautor had built and marketed a motorsailer, but it was a concept removed from the "performance/cruising" concentration of that company, and the model was later dropped in favor of more competitive designs. Nauticat picked up the molds and, turning to their in-house design team, now highly experienced in terms of the motorsailer, with assistance from Sparkman & Stephens as consultants, produced the 52 we are now discussing. The pedigree is good, and the yacht assuredly reflects this.

Although some may criticize her topside silhouette with house and high counter giving her a slightly "bow down" appearance when underway, the design is very subtle. The high "poopdeck" not only allows for a practical open cockpit with good deck access and full view ahead, but also furnishes full headroom in the after stateroom. The pilothouse also has ample headroom, two opening hatches through which the sails can be clearly seen, and a sensible view ahead from the steering station. When the starboard deckhead hatch is open the pilothouse engine instruments located over its windscreen can be comfortably monitored from the cockpit wheel.

This is an example of the seamanlike practices evident throughout this boat.

Since interior arrangements are, to a large extent, owner options, worked out in conjunction with Ted Cooper, of Nauticat USA in Marblehead, and the in-house design team in Finland, emphasis in this study is given to specific features and general quality of the standard production.

Without leaving the subject of owner options, both a happy owner and Ted Cooper were along on our sea trial. The owner had developed his detailed requirements with Ted, had been to the factory where they had been implemented conscientiously, and expressed himself as entirely satisfied with the treatment he had received. An important point. We feel anyone intending to spend the sort of money involved is entitled to a good deal of personal attention!

The pilothouse concept is one we particularly appreciate for cruising. It is often forgotten that, in many parts of the world, the weather at sea is not conducive to spending many hours in an open cockpit. This is applicable equally to the tropics and to cold climates. A summer day in the Chesapeake can prove an all-too-efficient substitute for the sauna, the only difference being the manner of cooking: one is broiled, not baked. For the liveaboard, the pilothouse provides an upper deck saloon that permits "lebensraum" in chilly weather as well as an excellent 360° view whatever the weather. Comfortable cruising time is thus extended in both spring and fall, with annual utilization of the vessel greatly increased in any one location. The beauty of this particular design is that both cockpit and pilothouse permit efficient and safe operation, which is not always true.

Deck layout is simple and practical. The Neco anchor windlass with remote control, heavy chain rodes and C.Q.R. anchors provide seamanlike ground tackle. Proper navigation lights are mounted on a substantial pulpit over the teak anchor platform, and a full teak rail with side opening gates runs the length of the vessel and gives a nice "big-ship" feel. The hatches are efficient; we can vouch for that, having had the same brand aboard our Monsun 31 sloop, but in our opinion they are a bit light for a vessel of this size, and effectively they need three hands to operate in a hurry—one for the latch and one each for the supports! They are also, regrettably, not "visitor proof"—i.e., guests not specifically instructed tend to do something silly, and strain them. On the same subject, while sails are stowed under the forecabin bunk, the hatch is too small for their bagged passage to the foredeck. There is a well-thought-through arrangement of mast pulpits, and life raft stowage ahead of these. Passage fore and aft along the deck is easy, with a step up to the poopdeck and comfortable and secure access to the cockpit from there.

The outside steering station is at the fore end of the cockpit, with the selftailing mainsheet winch in easy reach of the helmsman, and the genoa primaries, two healthy self-tailing Lewmar 65s, at the after end. This makes for an unusual tack as far as the helmsman is concerned—everything goes on behind him! He is left in peace to look where he is going.

Rig is, again, to some extent owner's choice. The yacht we sailed in had Hood Stoway electric furling main and SeaFurl genoa; the other one, which had arrived transAtlantic on its own bottom, had the standard conventional hoist and jiffy reefing. Standing rigging is very substantial—a double spreader rig on the main, a 10½" x 6½" aluminum extrusion stepped on the keel. The factory rig had 1 x 19 stainless to open bronze turnbuckles; lowers and intermediates were 12 mm (.47") to 18 mm (.7") turnbuckles.

Hood has substituted stainless Navtec turnbuckles but maintained the wire specs. However, the Hood mast step is secured with four galvanized carriage bolts of about ⅜". These were already rusty after less than one year in commission, and less than adequate in the first place. Aluminum and galvanized is a poor mix and seems ill-chosen underpinning for such expensive and sophisticated equipment.

The mizzen steps on a substantial block on the cockpit sole, well supported from below. The European-commissioned yacht had a Rotorstay doublegrooved roller furling headstay—again, substantial gear. Running backstay tackles are fitted for use when carrying spinnaker or large headsail.

It was a pleasure to see rigging designed not to reduce windage and fiddle about with an extra knot of speed, but rather to withstand the potential assaults of nature. A study of the rig failures in the recent Whitbread race will readily confirm this opinion.

Our sea trial was in stodgy New England fog, a useful challenge for the test of a cruising yacht. As was expected after the sight of the engineroom and acoustic shielding, the engine and generator starts produced little more than a comfortably reassuring throb. Quite the quietest yacht we have yet ridden. Full marks at last to a company that has woken up to the merits of effective acoustic protection. The hatch on the pilothouse sole has a buffer of 4½" thickness!

The single-screw model in which we ran had a left-handed propeller. Maneuvering was outstanding, and the hydraulic steering with back pressure relief valves was posi-

A motorsailer with the emphasis on the sail side of the equation, the Nauticat 52 has a tall, efficient sailplan on substantial aluminum spars and with seagoing specs for standing rigging and fittings.

tive and sensitive under power. A bit difficult to steady up "hands off" under sail, particularly in fog, but this criticism is marginal as the relative wind indicator was unserviceable, which meant "chasing" the compass. In spite of Marblehead's positive forest of yachts, moorings and lobster-pot buoys, complete confidence in the quick reaction of the yacht removed natural anxiety.

Making sail with the Hood gear "just happened!" I remain suspicious of this equipment for extended short-handed offshore passages in view of the possible problems arising in the event of failure, but this may well be tradition rampant (or perhaps the bias of an old man!). The convenience is remarkable. The main seemed a bit "flat" for the size and type of vessel.

Despite the light air—8-10 knots—the yacht moved well and tacked comfortably without much loss of way. This is the result of good underbody design and relatively heavy displacement (57,000 pounds, approximately).

We tested the auxiliary power from the optional generator sail-drive. Odd feeling: with the main engine off and no sails we ran at about 3 knots with good maneuvering speed from a mysterious source. The "S" drive is an original idea for emergency power; it has one great advantage which appeared particularly appropriate to our predicament of being surrounded by pot buoys in fog. If we got the main propeller fouled we still had both sail and power. Belt and braces plus!

Radar conning was simple, communication between radar and both wheel stations being easy. Obviously electronic and navigational equipment is owner's option and differed substantially on the two yachts inspected; the important point is that installations and wiring were good in both cases, and there is adequate space allowance for equipment and instrumentation.

On return to harbor we began our inspection of the yacht and its construction. Although both of the Nauticat 52s we inspected had been in service about a year, one had been commissioned at the factory and sailed transAtlantic, while the other had been commissioned in the U.S. and cruised in the islands. The Atlantic crossing had left no mark on the former, which was immaculate.

Ballast is external lead secured by 14 stainless keel bolts with heavy stainless backing plates. The hull-to-deck join is achieved by positioning screws and then bonding with multiple layers of fiberglass. The deck molding is stiffened by formed polyurethene foam-filled fiberglass beams. The teak is laid in a bedding of polysulfide and screwed through the solid fiberglass, then the screw ends are cut off, and additional lamination is run on the underside of the molding to insure watertight integrity. Windows are toughened safety glass in aluminum frames; storm boards are provided on request.

Interior construction is all wood. No fiberglass moldings are used. Plywood and laminates are preferred to solid timber. Teak veneers are agreeable, and the Resorcinol resins in the ply augur well for its longevity. As is to be expected in a Finnish vessel from the yard of a family of shipwrights, the standard of joinery is superior, and all visible screws were plugged. Floorboards of teak-veneered ¾" ply with inset finger pulls were a bit sloppy in one vessel, but better in the other.

Accommodation spaces were carefully finished, upholstery attractive, and bunks and seating comfortable with the single exception of the pilothouse settee on one vessel where the 4" foam sank below the high fiddle retaining the cushion, so that one's thighs were cut by the former.

In the model built for a European there were no fewer than four private double staterooms, each with its own head, which gives an idea of the big-ship feeling engendered by this vessel. Suitably equipped, she would make an ideal six-berth crewed charter yacht with the single reservation that her quality is such that it would be something like using a Mercedes as a rental car. The master staterooms were of different design, reflecting preferences of the two owners. One boasted an authentically Finnish sauna in place of the extra after guest cabin. As an old skiier from Little Finland in the Canadian Laurentians I could not fault it.

The galley in both vessels was excellent, with locker space outstanding. In one, a "pantry" outside the engineroom and adjacent to the galley supplied an especially commodious stowage area, the sort of convenience you take for granted in your

> Wisely, in our opinion, Siltala Yachts has remained faithful to its specialization, the building of efficient motorsailers...

The below-decks plan shown here represents only one of many possibilities. The Nauticat 52 is a semi-custom boat, and arrangements and furnishings are worked out by the Siltala design group to suit an owner's requirements.

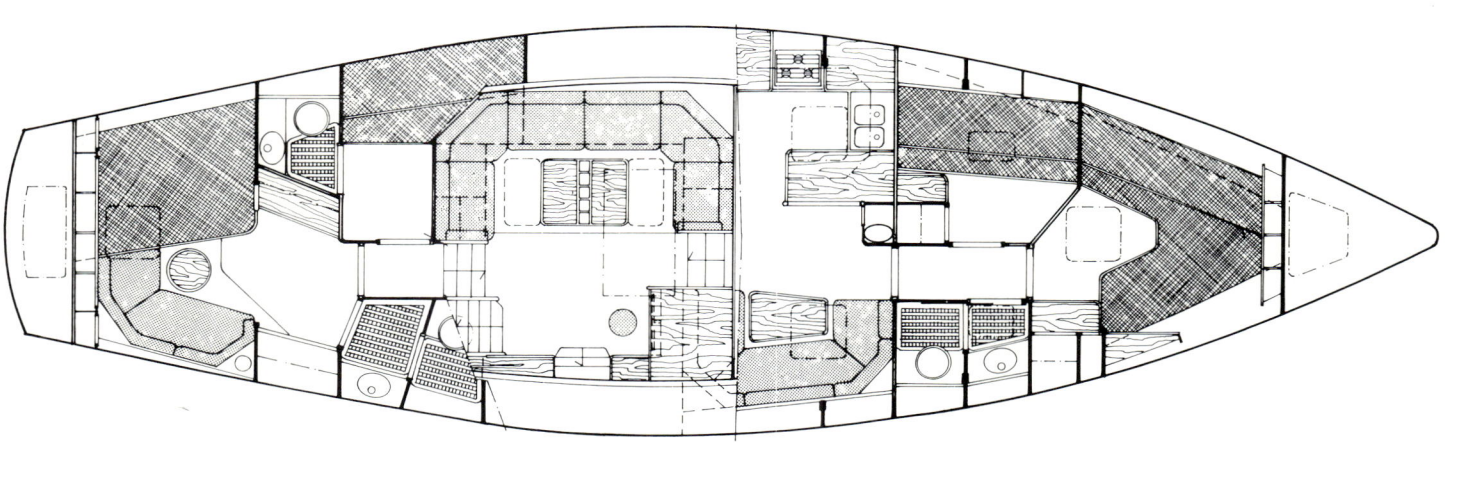

A lot of boat in a 51'2" x 15' package, the Nauticat 52 has a big, bright pilothouse with an efficient helm station and a U-shaped banquette for dining, chartwork or simply relaxing; another dinette below decks opposite the galley; a roomy vee-berth cabin forward; even an optional sauna. Elsewhere below there is space for two guest cabins with adjacent head/shower compartments, and an owner's cabin aft with a double berth.

LOA: 51'2"
LWL: 39'7"
Beam: 15'
Draft: 7'2"
Sail Area: 1371 sq. ft.
Ballast: 15,200 pounds
Displacement: 54,000 pounds
Fuel: 530 gallons
Water: 530 gallons
Power: Ford 2725E 6-cylinder diesel
Spars: aluminum
Hull: hand-layup solid fiberglass
Designer: Sparkman & Stephens/Siltala design group
Builder: Siltala Yachts Oy, Turku, Finland
Agent: Nauticat Inc., Box 809, Tucker's Wharf, Marblehead, MA 01945

castle but are surprised to find in 52 feet. We rejoiced in the under-counter toe-space allotted, and in the central serving counter with overhead cupboards opening from both sides. No complaints about the starboard dinette in either case; the only grumble is that the ports are too high for the average person. Ventilation was well planned, with ducts running to all accommodation spaces and supplied by a diesel fan heater. Hatches and ventilators were very adequate and air conditioning can be installed if required.

A minor criticism in the accommodation, probably resulting from the ship's construction in a northern climate, was that the cupboards were not ventilated top and bottom, and the ceiling planks were laid flush over the insulating material lining the hull. It is good practice to put about ½" spaces behind the planks and leave a sufficient gap at the base for condensation to run down into the bilge and not to the flats of bunks where it will cause damp mattresses.

The engineering in both boats was nicely done. In the single-engined version the Ford 2725E 6-cylinder diesel, developing 120 hp at 2500 rpm, was well mounted as was the Volvo diesel generator. Both were acoustically boxed and drew their air down 5" hoses. The outstanding result has already been mentioned. Ancillary equipment—bilge pumps, battery chargers, filters, etc.—were all well-mounted. Steel fuel tanks and stainless steel water-tank installations appeared satisfactory. Plumbing arrangements were good. We question the use of gate valves instead of seacocks which would be preferred on through-hull fittings, and on both boats numerous rusty hose clamps made by some company called Burlington came to our attention. They should be dismissed for supplying mild steel screws of low-grade rust resistance.

A steel flange attached to the steering yoke was rusting. In a vessel of this caliber bronze or stainless would seem obligatory. An emergency tiller was on board.

The electrical systems, distribution panels and cable runs were all of high quality. The batteries were well stowed, in a good covered box, forward of the mast under the passageway sole to port. The bus bars for the leads, however, were outside the box and unprotected. In this instance they were about to be shorted out by a very fancy chrome-plated barbecue stowed adjacent! Leads should be color-coded and connectors protected.

To conclude, such small deficiencies as have been mentioned, together with poor attention to good limber holes (a small compartment under the master stateroom aft was not limbered at all in either yacht) constitute minor defects such as we find on many boats. We contend that such apparently insubstantial flaws can sometimes generate a major crisis. They should be eliminated from scratch in yachts such as Nauticats, which aim with justification for the top of their market.

The wealth of knowledge and design philosophy built up within this company in the construction of these genuine oceangoing cruising yachts, coupled to the high standard of construction and joinery which one has come to expect from the Finns, in our opinion make the Nauticat 52 a fine possession for the year-'round cruising enthusiast or liveaboard.

····THE WORLD'S LIGHTEST MARINE DIESEL *by the designers of the Maybach Engines used in the* GRAF-ZEPPELIN····

The 80-foot Moano II owned by John W. Anderson of Detroit...Powered by two 150 h.p. MAYBACH DIESELS... now concluding her second season of continuous service.

Yachtsmen who are familiar with marine motors already understand that Diesels are not only far more economical in operation than gasoline engines, but that they are the most fool-proof and fire-safe power units known. ¶ These yachtsmen will be interested to learn that the same engineering organization which designed the MAYBACH ENGINES used in the famous GRAF-ZEPPELIN now offers a series of DIESEL ENGINES which are already establishing totally new standards in the powering of motor craft throughout the world. ¶ These MAYBACH MARINE DIESELS are the lightest weight engines per horsepower: comparatively small dimensions permit installation in boats as small as 45 feet; cost of operation is about one-third that of gasoline engines of similar ratings and their many refinements including vibrationless operation, reverse reduction gear (exclusive MAYBACH Patent) and bridge control make them unquestionably the outstanding engines in their specific field. ¶ Probably not more than thirty of these engines will be available for American installation next season. If you cannot visit our New York Headquarters, write us for the MAYBACH BOOK on DIESEL ENGINES.

F. W. von MEISTER
General Agent

578 Madison Ave.
New York City

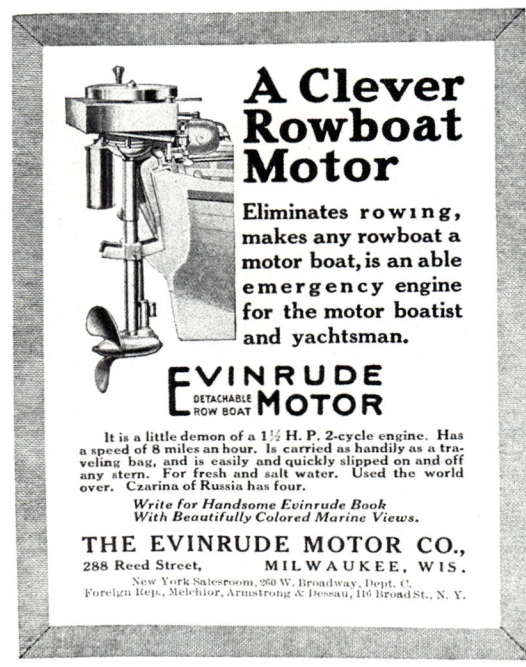

A Clever Rowboat Motor

Eliminates rowing, makes any rowboat a motor boat, is an able emergency engine for the motor boatist and yachtsman.

EVINRUDE DETACHABLE ROW BOAT MOTOR

It is a little demon of a 1½ H. P. 2-cycle engine. Has a speed of 8 miles an hour. Is carried as handily as a traveling bag, and is easily and quickly slipped on and off any stern. For fresh and salt water. Used the world over. Czarina of Russia has four.

Write for Handsome Evinrude Book With Beautifully Colored Marine Views.

THE EVINRUDE MOTOR CO.,
288 Reed Street, MILWAUKEE, WIS.
New York Salesroom, 250 W. Broadway, Dept. C.
Foreign Rep., Melchior, Armstrong & Dessau, 116 Broad St., N. Y.

Nothing *Finer* Can Be Said of Any Motor Boat Than, It is -

POWERED BY LYCOMING

LYCOMING MOTORS

LYCOMING MANUFACTURING CO.
WILLIAMSPORT, PENNSYLVANIA

SKIDOO!
MARINE ENGINE

The 2-Cycle-Engine-Sensation of the Year. Entirely new design introducing many exclusive features which challenge comparison with any other engine of its class, regardless of cost.

Pats. Pend.

Runs on Gasoline Distillate, Kerosene or Alcohol without change in equipment.

2 ACTUAL Bare H.P. Engine $23

COMPLETE ENGINE
With Fresh Water Boat Fittings . $39.90
With Salt Water Boat Fittings . 43.90

Weight, bare, 52 pounds; height from base 11¼ inches. Swiftest, most powerful, efficient and reliable engine of its size on earth. Drives Canoe, Rowboat or 14 to 20-foot Launch with load, 6 to 10 miles per hour. Easy to install and operate. Reversible—runs either way. Unfailing endurance powers—economical and safe—cannot back fire. Simple and compact in design, strong and durable in construction. Elevated, gearless commutator of special design, plunger pump without visible pipe connections, perfect lubrication. Highest grade material and workmanship.

Catalog FREE.

SOLD UNDER 5-YEAR GUARANTEE!

Belle Isle Motor Co., Dept. 24, DETROIT MICH.

The Geyer Reversible Propeller
Improved 1908 Model

Has Four Great Points of Advantage over all others:

(1) Increased Leverages
(2) Large Roll in Hub
(3) Keys instead of Pins, reducing Leverage
(4) Three Speeds both Forward and Reverse

Send for 1908 Illustrated Descriptive Circular

If you have used other makes you will appreciate these points or superiority.

MARINE HARDWARE CO.
PEABODY, MASS.

Winner of Chicago - Mackinac Endurance Race

THIS is the engine that won the long distance race from Chicago to Mackinac on July 20th, 1907, proving the endurance and reliability of our machine. We quote the following from a letter from the owner of "SWASTIKA," winner of the race:

"We are pleased to inform you that we won the Mackinac long distance race on July 20th, with our 42 x 10 motor boat "SWASTIKA" with your three-cylinder 16 H. P.

FAY & BOWEN ENGINE

We made the 332 miles in 36½ hours under rather trying conditions, such as heavy seas squalls, thick fogs, etc. Our boat was launched May 20th, and on the 21st without anyone in the crew that had had any experience with your engine, we started on our 200 mile trip to Chicago, which was made without any difficulties whatever."

We also build a successful kerosene engine   Write for catalogue of engines and boats

FAY & BOWEN ENGINE COMPANY,   -   -   115 Lake Street, Geneva, New York

THE MARINE ENGINE:
Its History Most Accurately And Entertainingly Presented

BY DONALD B. SHARP

Having accepted Adam's curse that "In the sweat of thy face shalt thou eat bread," people have since sweated just as much to ease the burden of earning a living. And having eased, they sweated even harder in pursuit of leisure, after which they sweated harder still to ease the labor of those pursuits until the agency of easy leisure became a pursuit in itself. Hence, all those engines in boats—originally a device to ease work, next one to enhance pleasure, and finally a pursuit in itself devoted to moving boats faster and faster just to prove that such a thing can be done. Thus, in few words, the socio-economic history of the marine engine. The details, however, take a little more telling.

In this discussion, "engine" means internal combustion, not steam. Despite the romance of glass-slipper launches with brass fittings, steam power offered little to the ordinary or slightly-more-than-ordinary yachtsman who ran his boat for the fun of it. A Gould or a Vanderbilt could afford 100 feet of steam yacht for the weekends or for the annual excursion to Maine, and a 100-footer could contain the boilers and machinery required to propel it, but people of lesser means had to be content with oars or sail or be crowded out of their own launch by a capacious boiler and a pile of firewood equally as big.

Writing in Rudder in 1896, Edward T. Birdsall declared: "One who has never been off for a day's pleasure in a small steam launch cannot imagine the amount of misery that one of these craft is capable of creating. The trip is usually extended beyond the capacity of the supply of fuel, with the result that the boat arrives home minus seats, lockers and floorboards."

Antique launch fanatics will now scream their objections, but Birdsall was right. Steam power served people who enjoyed fiddling with boilers and valves much more than it served people who wanted to go on simple nautical excursions. Those who went boating for the pleasure of the water had to wait for the compact convenience of internal combustion, which arrived only after a tortuous technical gestation preceded by numerous miscarriages and still births, and the first survivors of that gestation needed more mutations yet to assume a more-or-less standardized form.

THE FIRST FEW EXPLOSIONS

One curiosity of internal combustion power is that its earliest models offered to serve boats before land transport. This should be no surprise, for the Western Europe of, say, 1800, had more decent canals than roads. Given a means of motive power, people thought first of applying it to the faster, more effective means of transport.

Arguments persist about who did what first to develop internal combustion power, but the arguments can be put aside in favor of the word of C. Lyle Cummins, Jr., of the Cummins Engine Company family, as given in his exhaustive history of internal combustion, *Internal Fire* (Carnot Press: Lake Oswego, Oregon, 1976). Cummins notes Christian Huygen's experiments with a gunpowder engine in 1673, following which an Englishman, John Allen, filed a patent in 1729 proposing a gunpowder engine to force "...water or some other fluid through the stern or hinder part of a ship ... into the sea." Alas for Allen's proposal for the world's first (gunpowder-powered) jet boat, development of the steam engine—Savery, Newcomen, Watt, and all that—pushed internal combustion aside for a hundred-odd years. In 1827, Samuel Brown demonstrated a cruder internal combustion engine to the Lords of the Admiralty, running a 36' boat at about seven miles per hour on the Thames, so Brown gets the prize for the "first" marine engine even if the Sea Lords were not impressed (steam looked too promising).

The next documented experimenter was a Yankee, Samuel Morey, of Oxford, New Hampshire, a brilliant colonial who developed and tested a functional internal combustion engine in a 19' boat in 1829. Although steam dispossessed Morey of fame, he gets the credit for the first effective carburetor (and also the first flame arrester, much in its modern form).

Serious internal combustion marine power begins with Jean Joseph Etienne Lenoir's engines, circa 1860-1870. Like others of its era, Lenoir's engines were "atmospheric"—that is, they did not compress the air-fuel mixture prior to igniting it, and thus deprived themselves of the large release of energy that follows from compression of an air-fuel charge. Nonetheless, Lenoir produced engines for about ten years, and one 2-hp model drove a sort of water-taxi from Paris to Charenton for two years. Lenoir gets the prize for the first internal combustion marine engine that worked reliably enough to present an alternative to steam power.

Following Lenoir, another local boy, George Brayton, brought the Internal Combustion Cup home again. Brayton understood the benefits of compression, and he built an engine that used one piston to compress air-fuel, used another piston to exploit the expansion of the burning air-fuel charge, and used a continuous flame in the middle to ignite the charge on its way to the second, working piston. For this contribution—compression here, expansion there, and continuous combustion—Brayton gave his name to the modern gas turbine, which works in the same manner.

Brayton's engine was good enough (and he was hustler enough) to have several firms building versions of it around 1880, and Brayton put several into river boats, one a government boat moored at Exeter, New Hampshire. Cummins quotes an observer's assessment that the Brayton-powered boat was "... not a success, but it did run now and then with a great deal of coaxing." Within a few years, the successful four-stroke engines of Nicolaus Otto pushed Brayton's contender aside and returned the IC Cup to Europe (which must qualify as its permanent home, nothing having displaced Otto's cycle so far).

OTTO, DAIMLER AND MAYBACH

Nicholaus Otto's story deserves more telling than space allows. He was a man of genius who did not fully understand the dynamics of air and vaporized fuel that made his engines work, and he was dogmatic to the point of foolishness about defending the indefensible thermodynamics of his early experiments for the

> Those who went boating for the pleasure of the water had to wait for the compact convenience of internal combustion, which arrived only after a tortuous gestation...

sake of protecting his later patents. Yet he perceived the importance of compression prior to combustion and built engines that established the four cycles of intake, compression (and ignition), power, and exhaust that are familiar today.

Otto took the inspiration from Lenoir but got the money from Eugen Langen and, in 1864, the two formed a partnership that eventually became Klockner-Humboldt-Deutz AG. In 1872, Gottlieb Daimler joined the firm, bringing his protégé, Wilhelm Maybach, whom Cummins says became "the world's most renowned engine designer." In 1876, Otto came up with his four-cycle concept using compression, and in a single stroke he rendered all atmospheric engines obsolete. Like the fastest gun, he also gained a monopoly that was constantly challenged (and finally overcome), and which produced enmity that motivated his competitors when his patent was broken in 1886.

Daimler and Maybach, sharing some common enmity from corporate politics, left the Deutz group in 1882 to pursue their own design theories, particularly toward the purpose of powering vehicles, including boats. In 1886, they installed a two-cylinder, vee-type engine of 565-cc displacement in a launch. The engine had 100-mm-diameter pistons working through 60-mm strokes, and it developed 1.5 hp at 600 rpm. (Nowadays, a 565-cc outboard develops 40 hp.) In 1890, Maybach proved his genius again with what must have been the first in-line engine (cylinders arranged in a single row), a four-cylinder machine designed specifically for marine and industrial use. No matter that the engine only developed 5 hp, turned only 620 rpm, and weighed 330 pounds; this engine qualifies as the *ur*-engine of all marine powerplants that have come since. With its advent, a sort of marine die was cast.

Putting aside the issue of dates for the moment, Howard Greene wrote in Yachting in 1907: "In 1887...Gottlieb Daimler...used gasoline motors...for the propulsion of launches, with such success that they were introduced into this country in 1889. Daimler's early engines developed about 12 hp and weighed 1300 pounds. There were four tall cylinders—in fact, those very long cylinders were characteristic of the Daimler models, both afloat and ashore...and they brought the total height of the [12-hp] marine motor to 4 feet 4 inches. The floor space occupied was 2 feet 5 inches wide and 5 feet long."

> ...The awesome growth of the business literally provoked Yachting magazine into existence in 1907 and gave it a powerboat emphasis that it kept until the 1920s.

After contrasting this bulky Daimler to a "modern" 12-hp engine of 1907 that would weigh only "500 to 600 pounds," Greene added credit where due: "...the old Daimler was a great improvement on the steam power plants then used to produce the same amount of power, with their weight of at least 3 tons and their exorbitant demands for the best space. The installation of a Daimler engine meant practically the discarding of the weight of the boiler with its enormous added load of water and fuel..."

In this observation, Greene identified the direction of Maybach's genius: light weight as much as fuel efficiency and, since Daimler had his eye on a vehicle market, high (for those days) rotative speeds. Pursuit of these design goals defined engines for the 30 years following Maybach's 1890 prototype and still dominates engine design today.

Once Otto's patent was broken and once Maybach had set the pace, the engine world—mostly in Europe, but elsewhere, too—began to resemble a grade-school Easter egg hunt, with designers running off in all directions, some joining forces, others trading, and yet others stealing from unguarded baskets. The nearest similar thing of recent times was the proliferation of rented-garage and hip-pocket boatbuilders that sprang up to exploit fiberglass around 1960; but even that melee was tame compared to the engine ferment of 1900. French, British, and American licensees took up Daimler-Maybach designs, along with those of Otto, and pirates took advantage of every patent loophole that chauvinistic courts would allow. Meanwhile, Karl Benz in Germany and Charles Duryea in Massachusetts had demonstrated the utility of the horseless carriage, and the idea had been picked up with the greatest of enthusiasm by the French, e.g., Panhard, Lavassor, Delahaye, Peugeot, Renault, DeDion, and Darracq, to name a few who had their feet firmly in the burgeoning automobile world but were as eager to see how fast a boat could go under power. In the May, 1905, issue of Rudder, W. P. Stephens marveled: "One would hardly believe that any other form of sport could displace automobile racing in France, and yet the events scheduled in the nautical calendar exceed in number and importance those planned for the road, and they are attracting quite as much public attention."

Stephens went on to describe a four-cylinder Delahaye with 12-inch pistons working through 8¾-inch strokes, developing 300 hp at 700 rpm, and weighing 2500 pounds. (A modern engine of similar 3956 cubic inches, or 65 liters, displacement would develop nearer to 2500 hp.) This particular Delahaye counters the notion of a lightweight marine engine, but it indicates the extremes of the era in the pursuit of speed and large cash purses on the water.

AMERICAN ENTERPRISE

If Europeans went to extremes to compete for $22,000 (1905 dollars) in prizes at Monaco, America was the democracy of the working man, and practically every blacksmith shop in the northeast and in the Chicago-Detroit crescent set up to build marine engines. Indeed, the awesome growth of the business literally provoked Yachting magazine into existence in 1907 and gave it a powerboat emphasis that it kept until the 1920s. It also provoked the organization of the National Association of Engine and Boat Manufacturers (which listed 52 active members in 1907), and led to the first New York Boat Show in 1905. The names have the ring of a long time ago—Speedway, Williamson, Victor, Royal, Standard, Craig, Jager, Rochester, Belle Isle, St. Clair, Ferro, Fay and Bowen, Doman, Boothbay, United, Lozier, Clifton, Hasbrouck, Sterling, Ralaco, Buffalo, Monarch, Termaat and Monahan, Stanley, American, Murray and Tregurtha, Bridgeport, Strelinger—but forbear! Enough, and the list is not half done. The modern boat owner has only a fraction as many names to choose from, for when the European notion of marine power emigrated, it came with the conviction of a Jesuit missionary and the force of a plague.

That long, though incomplete, list raises the question of what became of so many brand names. In fact, many simply weren't good enough to survive or were built by modest or backward enterprises that could not improve them as fast as the competition. As with tabletop computers today, when hordes of eager young engineers find themselves on the frontier of a new technology and find their efforts blessed by a ready market, technical improvements come fast, and when the technology settles down to a routine, its pioneering path will be littered with those who couldn't keep up (and those who managed to make a fast buck and got out early).

A reasonable question somewhere along here is: Why didn't the fast-growing U.S. marine world look to the car world for its engines, as it does today? The answer is that domestic car engines weren't good enough. In France and Germany, the automobile served the wealthy and was built to justify the prices they paid, so every one of the French engines cited earlier had an automotive background. By contrast, even the domestic luxury cars of, say, 1905, were notoriously unreliable in operation and prone to catastrophic failure. In sum, not only did the marine world get internal combustion first but, up to about 1930, it also got the best of its engineering.

As everyone knows, at 60 mph, the 200-hp engine in a car may be developing only 50 hp. By contrast, a marine engine runs at close to full output all the time with corresponding requirements for quality. Of course, engine manufacturers had a lot of help from the fallacious "truism" that "weight doesn't matter in a boat," so they poured enough cast iron into engine blocks and crankshafts to be proof against failure. They also got a lot of help from the sustained-speed mode of marine operation. Early automotive engines suffered from the primitive systems used to accommodate their fuel-supply and ignition components to throttle-up, throttle-down, stop-and-go driving. By contrast, the more constant speed marine engine had less trouble of this sort. In time, some engines from the automotive world—Winton, Simplex, Lozier, and Kermath, to name a few—did earn enviable reputations on the water. But, in general, the automotive engine offered little to the marine world until after 1930. In more time (to get slightly ahead of the story), automotive engines became so good and so low-priced that they drove out the venerable names—Standard, Mianus, Scripps, Erd, Sterling, Hall-Scott, to name a half-dozen—that graced the classic days of marine power.

To indulge a digression on the theme of mortality, internal combustion also laid to rest the hopes of Frank W. Olfeldt, inventor of the naphtha- and alcohol-vapor engines patented in 1883 and 1887. Stated simply, these were fully-condensing Rankine (e.g., steam) engines that used alcohol or naptha, rather than water, as a working fluid. Birdsall, our cynical observer from the pages of Rudder, foresaw a great future for vapor engines, noting in 1896 that "Few meritorious inventions...have been brought to perfection in such a short time...." Alas, these "perfect" vapor engines were effectively gone within five years.

FUELING AND FIRING

To return to the technical problems of early engines, today hardly anyone gives a carburetor or ignition system a second thought. They are just there, need a little maintenance now and again, but are otherwise unremarkable. By contrast, engines of 1900 had no standardized system for mixing fuel with air and no standardized system for setting the mixture on fire, the fuel-mixing problem being compounded by the lack of a fuel of consistent volatility and specific gravity. Indeed, in the earliest era of internal combustion, users on the West Coast sometimes specified fuel from a particular oil well to guarantee themselves a consistent product.

In a 1905 issue of Rudder, E. W. Roberts described four common air-fuel mixing devices, noting that, of the four, "carburetors are nowadays very little used," and suggesting the state of the art with this advice: "In a small boat where the movement of a person from the stern to the bow will cause considerable change of trim it will be necessary to open the needle valve slightly before going forward."

The state of things is further indicated by the fact that in 1907 the United Manufacturing Company, of Detroit, Michigan, sold its 8-hp Little Giant motor "bare" for $87. Having bought the Little Giant, the customer bought an ignition system and fuel mixer elsewhere, perhaps paying as much as $18 for, for instance, a suitable Schebler carburetor. As late as 1915 a carburetor (or other fuel-mixing device) was not standard equipment on all engines.

Things were little better in the fuel-igniting department, with make-and-break, high-tension, and magneto systems contending for eminence. The earliest ignition systems used a "hot tube" which was stuck through the top of

> In a 1905 issue of Rudder, E.W. Roberts described four common air-fuel mixing devices, noting that, of the four, "carburetors are nowadays very little used…"

the cylinder. An open flame (hardly well-advised, given the volatile fuels of the day) heated the external end of the tube, thus keeping the internal portion hot. At some point as the piston moved upward on its compression stroke, the hot tube ignited the air-fuel mixture much as overheated spark plugs cause a modern automobile with pollution controls to continue to run raggedly after the ignition has been shut off. The combustion point was dictated by assorted variables—mixture, air temperature, engine temperature—and could not be controlled for optimum power or fuel economy, nor could the system achieve high rotative speeds. The early engineers threw away hot-tube ignition as soon as electrical ignition systems were available.

Electrical systems brought spark plugs and all that ails them, plus batteries that go dead and wiring that gets wet. Make-and-break systems used movable contacts within the cylinder that opened and closed to create a low-voltage spark. High-tension systems, which became the norm after about 1910, used conventional spark plugs and induction coils. Both systems might use dry-cells or wet batteries; if dry-cells died at sea, skippers were advised to punch the zinc cases full of holes and immerse them in salt water to restore them enough to limp home. Freshwater skippers, of course, had to paddle. Alternately, magnetos were made in low- and high-tension forms and Yachting and Rudder, circa 1910, ran articles arguing the merits of each and advising how to keep them working.

TWO-STEP, FOUR-STEP

Just as the technology of 1905 had not worked out a decent fuel or ignition system, it had not made up its mind about two-cycle (e.g., modern outboards and Detroit diesels) or four-cycle (e.g., everything else) systems. A four-cycle system requires movable valves that open at the right time relative to piston motion to admit air-fuel and to release exhaust. The simpler two-cycle system, á la the outboard, uses atmospheric pressure to fill the crankcase with air-fuel, then uses a counterweight on the crankshaft to shove the air-fuel charge through a port into the cylinder. Exhaust gas escapes through its own port due to its own expansion. Two-cycle makes possible simplicity, light weight, and high rotative speeds, but at some cost to fuel economy. Simplicity—and, thus, reliability—mattered most in 1900 and virtually all the smaller marine engines were two-cycle. They look "cute" today, with their round, bulbous crankcases, usually built up in sections rather than cast in one piece, and with their tall, one-piece cylinders, often with intake and exhaust pipes mounted one above the other. As long as the leather or marline crankcase seals held up, they ran as well as free-surface carburetors and make-and-break ignition would allow.

If two-cycle engines of, say, 1905, look "cute," the four-cycle engines of the era look like Rube Goldberg's first effort. Pushrods, valves, and valve springs are exposed; oil-drip cups abound with external oil tubes running to bearings; carburetors mount in impossible locations; connecting rods may be exposed; and even enclosed crankcases have inspection ports for regular tightening of connecting-rod bearings.

The diesel engine fits in here somewhere, although it was preceded by the "oil engines" that C. Lyle Cummins calls an "interim" solution, the interim being the time after gasoline engines were fairly reliable and before diesels were even available.

Today, with octane ratings on every service-station gasoline pump by federal edict, no one can appreciate the varied quality of the fuels that were offered to the engine designer or power-boat owner of 1900. Indeed, St. Clair Motor Company, of Detroit, Michigan, advertised in Yachting that its 2-hp Skipper would run on kerosene, distillate oil, alcohol, or gasoline. Given that the oily leftovers from refining gasoline were cheap, and that they presented little or no fire hazard, oil engines enjoyed some popularity. Some used fuel pre-heaters or complex atomizers to get the fuel into a combustible form and used hot tubes or sparks for ignition. Others were diesel precursors in the respect that they depended on the heat generated by compression for ignition.

In 1901, J.W. Eaton somewhat smugly declared in Rudder that: "The use of gasoline and naphtha has probably reached its highest point in development... It is certain that the kerosene motor is destined to occupy a very high place in the generation of power in the future."

Having so declared, Eaton went on to describe an engine wherein kerosene was drawn into a heated plenum of sorts—a virtual pre-combustion chamber á la the modern diesel—and ignited apparently from both the heat of the plenum and the heat from compression.

Eaton's technical explanation is about as good as his prognostication (unless his prediction be allowed to encompass diesels), so details remain obscure; yet he effectively described the diesel injection system of the era, wherein fuel was forced into the cylinders by air pressure developed by an ancillary pump. The difficulties of the system, plus the weight of metal needed to contain diesel working pressures, kept diesels out of boats until James McKechnie's unit injector of 1910 refined fuel metering to the point that diesels could be built in small sizes. However, air-injection diesels survived for 20 years up to the 1930s.

Prior to 1912, Yachting listed Mianus, Nlseco (New London Ship and Engine Company), and Charles L. Seabury Company as diesel manufacturers, but provided no details. In 1912, J.T. Rowland recalled in Yachting that Roald Amundsen pulled the steam engine out of Fridtjof Nansen's old Colin-Archer-designed *Fram* and put in a diesel engine before going off to the South Pole, then described the 108′ 10″ LWL schooner *Orion,* which had just received a

> ...If dry-cells died at sea, skippers were advised to punch the zinc cases full of holes and immerse them in salt water to restore them enough to limp home.

60-hp diesel that was said to be reversible. In the same year, Yachting devoted several paragraphs of boat-show news to the Mietz and Weiss oil engines and, in 1916, devoted one paragraph to the Nlseco family of diesels. Apparently, diesels were of little importance to Yachting's readers until around 1930, about the time Cummins Engine Company shifted some of its marketing effort from commercial to yacht applications.

GEARS AND PROPELLERS

Obviously, engine propulsion called for a means of transmitting power to the water, plus some means of arresting the flow of power and reversing it at will. Steam engines could be pretty easily reversed and so required no form of transmission. Two-cycle gasoline engines could be reversed by first turning off the ignition, then turning it back on during the last, dying turn of the crankshaft; but, if done ineptly, the engine re-started and ran forward, or "go ahead," as was said, with resultant damage to boats, piers, and the helmsman's self-esteem. Four-cycle engines could not be depended upon to reverse themselves at all.

The marine transmission, then, developed along with the engine. Most were planetary gear systems with inner workings similar to those of a modern Borg-Warner or Paragon gear, but wrought with a long control lever. Shifting one of Joe's Famous Reversing Gears, from the Snow and Petrelli works, called for as much as a 70-pound pull on a four-foot lever if the gear were matched to a large engine. Despite their awkwardness, such gears served well enough, for they were not significantly refined until the Paragon hydraulic gear of the late 1940s.

For years, the way out of the awkwardness of a gearbox was the reversing propeller, a system that seems almost innocent today and the very existence of which betrays the modest output and rotative speeds of the engines it (sort of) served. These propellers were mounted on a large, hollow shaft that had a control rod running through it to alter the pitch of the propeller blades for maximum advance, no

> Propellers themselves were the products of virtual cut-and-try science, despite close to a hundred years (in 1900) of experimenting with steamship screws...

advance (neutral), or reverse. In an era of primitive carburetors wherein many engines ran at only one speed, such feathering propellers provided speed control through variable pitch.

Some peculiarly optimistic expressions of the idea resembled two propellers mounted on the same shaft, one behind the other. In neutral, the blades opposed each other to maintain the load on the engine so that it didn't run away with itself—another reminder of the inability to control engine speed. The Roper Safety Propeller people, around 1907, made much of how the system achieved reliability through reduced shock when changing direction and ran dramatic advertisements showing a wholesome suburban family threatened from ahead, abaft, and abeam by steamships and sailing yachts, but presumably saved from disaster by their Roper propeller—saved because they didn't have to depend on getting an engine to reverse itself. As Yachting's commentator promised: "It ...is so reliable in every emergency and so simple and easy and yet sure in operation that women can with safety and confidence manage the motor boat equipped with one."

Male chauvinism aside, certainly few women would have enjoyed the 70-pound pull needed to shift one of Joe's gears. Such propellers as the Roper must have been hideously inefficient, given the size of the hub, but they remained in use until around 1930. Nowadays, editors of boating magazines get frequent inquiries from hopeful readers who have "heard about" some wonderful feathering propeller, the inquirers (and the editors) not knowing that such propellers couldn't handle more than around 50 hp at about 400 rpm and so disappeared as power and speed increased. Feathering propellers for boats do remain today, as do their efficiency losses and power limitations.

Propellers themselves were the products of virtual cut-and-try science, despite close to a hundred years (in 1900) of experimenting with steamship screws. After considerable research, even William Froude, the English experimenter, could not tie down the hydrodynamics of a propeller. Propeller designers guessed and hoped, and boating writers evaded the issues or perpetrated errors of understanding. For example, in 1908, Yachting's Phillip J. Overman ascribed the "squat" of a launch stern to displacement of water by the propeller, but paid no attention to the contribution of the wave system set up by the hull itself, nor showed any awareness of the crucial relationship of power to propeller pitch to so-called "hull speed." To the modern eye, the blades of early propellers look too narrow to develop good thrust, so Overman may have had a point; such propellers would do a great deal of threshing under the counter without creating much forward push.

HULL-DESIGN FOR POWER

The propeller business reminds that the whole propulsion system must be rationalized for the hull; and if propeller science was cut-and-try, powerboat hull design was cut-and-hope, certainly for "speed" hulls. The steam launches, with their length-to-breadth ratios of 5:1 or more provided a poor starting point, but designers used it anyway. The French 12-meter power launches of 1905, when "12-meter" meant around 40 feet, typically had a beam of around five feet. Thus, even the 90' *Gregory* of 1905, powered by twin Standard gasoline engines of 300 hp at 400 rpm, had a beam of only 12 feet. With 4000 gallons aboard, *Gregory* was reckoned to have a range of 1400 miles at her top speed of 23 mph (at a reported fuel consumption of 60 gallons per hour).

To digress briefly (upon this cogent exemplar) *Gregory* made quite a name for herself with a non-stop, maiden passage from New York to Sevastopol, during which she survived a hurricane that put her several hundred miles off course. She arrived without needing to refuel on the way and became the oft-cited inspiration of naval officers eager to escape the constraints of coal-fired steam power—particularly the telltale stream of black smoke.

Powerboats had no more than appeared before well-heeled gentlemen began racing them and designers soon learned that speed was a matter of planing, and that planing depended on flat bottom sections, and that flat bottoms brought pounding that could be ameliorated by a pronounced vee in forward sections that made a careful transition to a flat bottom aft. Given 50-hp engines that weighed 500 pounds, or 200-hp engines that weighed more than a ton, however, the first powerboat designers chose long, narrow launch-type hulls in an effort (possibly misguided) to minimize wetted area at speed. They were beginning to develop modern planing-powerboat hulls, and they began with sailing and steam launch models that were something else entirely. The reason they did not invent the modern deep-vee planing hull was not that they did not know how; rather, they didn't have the engines to push such resistant hulls. But they achieved spectacular results with such boats as *Dixie Junior* of 1912, which her design firm, Tams, Lemoine and Crane, guaranteed to make 35 mph with a six-cylinder Sterling rated for a maximum 90 hp at 1200 rpm. This gentleman's speedboat cost $4500, or about eight years' wages for a $50-a-month semi-skilled factory worker. A Cigarette of today, fully-prepared for offshore racing, will cost proportionally as much and will make 90 mph with 1000 hp.

Where designers did not seek speed, they too easily contented themselves with variations on the steam-launch theme or with sail hulls shorn of rigging. Even so notable a figure as Norman L. Skene, writing in Rudder in 1905, could not produce a coherent theory of powerboat hull design. The question of the optimum stern got far too much attention to the neglect of the overall design, an emphasis to suggest that designers were so concerned about why the

> ...Both Rudder and Yachting ran articles advising the sailing skipper how to get an engine into a sailboat and how to get along with it once it was there.

stern squatted that they failed to wonder why the bow lifted. For example, *Ildico III*, a 45' launch of 1907 (built as tender for racing sloops wonderfully named *Attila* and *Hun*), shows a deep forefoot and full underbody back to amidships (apparently to support the engine), but a peculiarly rising run aft. The stern would have been saved from squatting only by wide, flaring buttock lines. In general, Edwardian powerboats were either displacement launches or planing raceboats, with little in between. However, even by 1908, the semi-displacement hull that could make good use of heavy, low-horsepower engines had appeared in the San Francisco area, the 53' *Lillian* being notable because "her extreme beam is carried well aft," as Charles Royce Barney noted in Yachting, along with the observation that she was a "compromise between a speedboat and a cruiser." The "cruiser" part implies a full-displacement hull of the launch type.

Of course, if "yachting" rather meant powerboats in those days, this hardly ended the matter, for the sailing world could enjoy motoring through a calm as much as they do now. Thus, in 1901, the fishing schooner *Ruth E. Pember*, 110' LOA, got an engine of 50 hp at 300 rpm that turned a propeller 44 inches in diameter and with 50 inches of pitch—hardly a wholesome pitch-diameter ratio by contemporary standards. But assuming 30 percent slip, it must have given her about 10 mph, and it probably worked reliably enough to push her in and out of Fulton Market. Auxiliary power for sailing vessels was not reserved for commercial boats in the early years of the century; both Rudder and Yachting ran articles advising the sailing skipper how to get an engine into a sailboat and how to get along with it once it was there. When power came to boating, no one got left out. Yachting even noted engines that could be installed in canoes, and gave complimentary notice to the outboards of Evinrude and Waterman when they arrived. Evinrude advertised his 1¾-hp wares as "row boat" motors or as "get home" power, proudly noting that the Czarina of Russia had four for her private yacht.

END OF THE BEGINNING

If power came to American boating in 1889 (per Greene), the whole institution was in place by 1900 and was thriving by 1905. Yachting's Henry Irving estimated that residents of New York State owned 12,000 power boats in 1907; the editors quoted a manufacturer who reported having sold 5000 engines up to 1907 and who expected to sell as many that year alone. The Palmer Engine Company of Cos Cob, Connecticut, said they had sold 35,000 engines by 1909. Commodore Henry L. Hertz, of the Pistakee (Wisconsin) Yacht Club wrote glowingly: "The motor boat invasion...has developed a new fever among the summer resorters....Young girls, boys, women, young and old, as well as men of all degrees, handle motor boats of high and low power with the assurance of veterans...I would not dare to say how many motor boats I saw...last summer... you would accuse me of exaggeration...the growth of the sport in the West is the healthiest thing I know of. I believe the great decrease in mortality...and consequent increase in general health of the people can be traced in a great degree to this cause." Not even the most enthusiastic—or highly-paid—public relations agent of today would dare claim such a thing.

Just as the harnessmaker regarded the new-fangled automobile with suspicion, so did the licensed steamboat operators cast wary orbs on internal-combustion-powered boats. Earlier, they had tried and failed to bring vapor launches under their licensing programs, and they tried again with internal combustion. Much of the early zeal for motorboat registration and regulation came from steam engineers who disliked seeing their monopoly broken. The steam operators pushed their interests too far, though, until it collided with that of the commercial fishing skippers. Fishing skippers often shipped foreign or immigrant crews, but the steam interests sought to restrict licensing to "Americans" who were "well paid." Yachting, viewing this attitude as sensible and patriotic, since the Navy would depend upon the fisheries for competent seamen in time of war, felt that "low class foreigners, who were willing to work for little and live like swine," would hardly make fitting defenders of the country. Nonetheless, the licensing laws, such as were proposed, exempted the fishing fleet and their "low class" crews, and federal laws affecting powerboats were delayed until 1940, although states did pass registration and numbering laws.

Despite the caprice of the engines of the time, despite marginal understanding of powered hulls, despite conflicting interests, the powerboat was fully arrived by 1910—despite, as A. E. Potter noted, in Yachting in 1907, those: "croakers who decry the advent of the power boat...who, around the club house and grounds, object strenuously to ill-smelling exhaust and the grime-covered habiliments of those whom they counted as friends until they forfeited such esteem by 'falling from grace,' which is to say, buying gasoline engines and 'smoke' boats or 'put puts.'"

Indeed, perhaps something was lost when powerboats appeared at the yacht-club docks— but much was gained, too.

THE MACHINERY MATURES

The engines of the first 20 years—1890 to 1910—made a haphazard lot, a confusion of quality wherein some, such as Standard and Scripps, represented the best engineering of the day while others represented expedient, *ad hoc* efforts for quick profit. In the next 20 years— 1911 to 1931—the weak and the aloft-by-night disappeared, the serious men of affairs took control, and marine engines became second

> Despite the caprice of the engines of the time, despite marginal understanding of powered hulls, despite conflicting interests, the powerboat was fully arrived by 1910...

only to aircraft engines in quality. Indeed, in some instances, particularly following WWI, they were the same engines.

The technical improvements of the era are "ho-hum" stuff today. Lubrication via pump rather than oil-drip cups, for example, and water-cooled exhaust manifolds. Fairbanks-Morse added a system for using manifold heat to pre-heat intake air, a recognition of the fuels of the day and of all-weather use of engine power. Leary two-cycle engines of 1912 had two carburetors per cylinder, the second one contributing only at high speed in the manner of the secondary throats of a modern "four-barrel" carburetor. Trebert came close to a record for low pound-per-hp ratios with a 100-hp V8 that weighed only 540 pounds; this engine, for the racing crowd, had a peculiar anticipation of radial aircraft-engine construction wherein the connecting rod big end of one bank encircled the crankshaft, and the big end of the corresponding rod on the opposite bank attached to the big end of the main rod. The engine qualified as "valveless" in the terminology of the day, since it did not use conventional poppet valves, but had a form of slide valve that moved back and forth across a cylinder port, up to admit fuel-air, down to allow exhaust to escape. The exhaust pipes, one for each cylinder, extended vertically above the engine, the "stacks" visible in some of the old pictures.

One curiosity of the engines of this second era is their varied provenance. Many were auxiliary power units from farm and factory, these being the simpler, heavier, and cheaper of the choices. In 1912, Loew-Victor sold a 60-hp-at-1300-rpm four for as little as $850. (By contrast, a 55-hp Jager cost $2800.) Otherwise, the developing aircraft industry, mostly in the form of Elbridge, which claimed to be the leading airplane engine in the mid-teens, entered the marine market, both with engines and with a deadly 140-mph iceboat driven by an elevated engine and airplane propeller, á la the "airboats" of the Florida Everglades.

The Wright brothers' shop, Wright Aeronautical, sold one of their V-12 Typhoon engines— 5.75-inch stroke, 1047 cubic inches, and 550 hp at 1900 rpm (2100 rpm, maximum)—to Richard F. Hoyt, a New Yorker in a hurry, who put it in his *Teaser,* in which he commuted from Long Island and with which he made the Albany-New York run on the Hudson in better time than the Twentieth Century Limited. Thus encouraged, Wright put the engine into the New York Boat Show in 1926—price not specified.

The Typhoon did not become a standard boat-show item, and in a few more years Wright merged with its long-time arch-rival Curtiss. Perhaps the Typhoon's best shot came in *Horace,* Horace E. Dodge's (as in Dodge Brothers automobiles) flagship for his Watercar line of boats. Dodge ill-advisedly sought to create a family of runabouts, á la Chris-Craft and Gar Wood, but despite Yachting's assertion (1927) that Watercars were "increasing in popularity," Dodge's marine venture lasted only a few years. The early Watercars used standard Dodge automobile engines (except for the 50-mph, Typhoon-powered *Horace*) and no one found reason to object. The last Watercars used Lycoming engines, but not from the aircraft side of the house.

Elsewhere, Herr Maybach's business had recuperated from the Great War and was supplying 12-cylinder, 600-hp engines for such vehicles as the Graf Zeppelin. Charles N. Edge preferred the Maybach engine for his *Dorica,* with which he commuted to Wall Street from Rye. While the 600-hp Maybach got the attention at the New York Boat Show in the mid-'twenties, a more important product was a "lightweight," 150-hp "high-speed" diesel— no details given. Such an engine deserved more notice, even if it wasn't enough for *Dorica*.

Other engines, such as Sterling and Scripps, were originally marine engines, Sterling having made its name in the *Dixie* series of hydroplanes and in races where Scripps had been a prime competitor. Racing aside, Scripps clearly took the 1912 prize for price, its 105-hp six selling for $3500. By 1925, the price of a 100-hp Scripps E-6 engine was down to $1750; but in 1926 Henry Ford sold new Model T Fords for $290 each and a semi-luxury Willys-Knight sedan cost only $1575.

Besides from farm and airfield, marine engines also came from the railroads. The Hall-Scott Motor Car Company did not make automobiles; rather, they made engine-driven railcars. Likewise, besides cars, Winton built engines for switching locomotives, and the memory of Winton rail and marine engines survives in the ElectroMotive Division (EMD) of General Motors, which bought Winton in 1932. Alco, or American Locomotive, was slower to enter the marine world, but is now the standard alternative to an EMD marine engine.

FROM ST. CLAIR'S SHORES

The shadow over the New York Boat Show of 1912, the cloud no bigger than a man's hand, came from an upstart, Kermath, a builder of automotive engines. Seeking to reassure doubtful buyers about a question that still comes up today, *Yachting*'s evaluator declared that "the Kermath is essentially a marine, rather than an automobile motor," for which falsehood the commentator may be excused; less excusably, the commentator did not perceive the implications of a marine engine from the mass-production automobile industry.

The fruition of the implications has been suggested in reference to Dodge's Watercars. Shortly after Dodge's arrival, Chrysler (which did not yet own Dodge) created a Marine Division and offered the original six-cylinder Crown, plus the Imperial eight. The Crown had several notable features which showed that the automobile industry was catching up to marine-engine builders; it had an integral intake and exhaust manifold, for pre-heating of intake air; fuel pump on the engine rather than remote; dual downdraft carburetors, aluminum pistons, and seven main bearings on the crankshaft, each connecting rod having a main bearing on each side. The Chrysler Crown was a fine piece of 1930 work and its later mutations remained in production past 1970.

If Chrysler's entry were not enough, the automobile contribution was even more evident in the 1931 New York Boat Show. *Yachting*'s observer reported: "The next thing that caught the eye was a white-painted, aluminum-cased, Lodge 4-40. Anyone who has looked under the hood of a Ford car was quick to recognize the cylinder block...In general, the fittings of this engine are standard Ford parts..."

The engine was that of the Model A, the improved successor to the Model T. It was a retrograde, job-lot design with nothing but cheapness and simplicity to recommend it to the non-demanding and non-discriminating; its importance in 1931 lies with the Lodge element: an independent marinizer developing a marine version of a cheap, mass-produced engine of sufficient quality to satisfy most boating needs. Hence, 50 years later, the Outboard Marine Corporation, MerCruiser, Crusader, et al., are marinizers who re-do G.M. engines, while PleasureCraft and Commander, et al., do Fords.

RATIONAL NUMBERS

This is getting somewhat ahead of the story, for the marine engine industry had most of 1911-1931 all to themselves, and they created some of the best engines of the time (and some of the most expensive, too). However, to the

> ...The marine engine industry had most of 1911-1931 all to themselves, and they created some of the best engines of the time (and some of the most expensive, too).

modern eye, those engines have strange specifications: 1300 rpm qualifies as "high speed" in 1920, while racing engines of 1980 run at 5500 rpm. Cylinder bores run around five inches in 50-100-hp engines, and pistons strokes run six, whereas four-and-four indicate a "big" machine by modern standards. The 125-hp, six-cylinder Buffalo, a true trawler-shrimper engine, had a 10-inch bore, a 12-inch stroke, a maximum speed of 300 rpm, and an idle speed of 100 rpm—slow enough to watch. It also weighed 11,000 pounds; its four-cylinder, 85-hp brother weighed 7300 pounds—it took 3700 pounds to add two more cylinders.

Bore, stroke, rpm, and weight get attention here because their relationship to each other in the 1911-1931 era betray the constraints upon engine design that were imposed by the fuels of the day. The two spark plugs per cylinder in a 1928 Karmath 125-hp six or a Sterling Petrel six do not prove that the power is particularly sophisticated or hairy-chested; the designer simply had to use two plugs to get the fires going inside.

To back up one step, compression ratio defines the ratio of the volume of the cylinder with the piston all the way down (bigger number) to the volume with the piston all the way up (given as 1); for example, modern V8 engines have a compression ratio of around 8.5:1. The greater the compression ratio, obviously, the more the fuel-air charge is compressed before ignition and the more heat it releases upon combustion.

Alas for efficiency, once compression ratio goes much above 6:1, heat from compression will ignite a gasoline-air mixture; hence, "knock," which is an explosion rather than a controlled burning and which, when severe, can blow a cast iron cylinder head off an engine. Thus, early engine designers seeking more power could not, as they would have liked, simply raise compression ratio to some suitable maximum because the fuels of their day had no anti-knock ingredients. The octane scale itself was not devised until 1926, although General

Motors and Standard Oil did combine trade secrets in 1924 to sell tetraethyl lead through the Ethyl Corporation. But tetraethyl lead did not solve all the problems at once, and engine designers had to fill the years up to 1924 with something.

Stymied at high compression ratios as a means of increasing output, engine designers could choose between adding cylinders or making cylinders bigger. Fewer big cylinders reduced the total of parts, but imposed rpm limitations because of the weight of the reciprocating pistons and connecting rods; likewise, the very bulk of cast iron needed to surround large pistons and contain long strokes brought weight. The good news was that big-bore, long-stroke, low-rpm engines were well suited to driving propellers, often without reduction gears and their attendant (slight) parasitic power consumption.

Note where all this points: as soon as designers got high-compression fuels, and as soon as the automobile industry discovered the marine industry and decided to dispose of its surplus there, things were going to change. Except for the Depression and WWII, the change would have come much sooner. As things happened, it had to wait for the first generation of high-speed (4500 + rpm) automotive V8 engines of the 1950s.

DIESELS DEVELOP

Gasoline power was not all. In 1919, Clessie L. Cummins began building what must be the first truly home-grown American diesels, and he enjoyed singular success selling them into heavy workboats and fishing vessels. By the late 1920s, Cummins had become a visible entity in the yachting world. Speedway, Hall-Scott, Standard, and Winton got into diesel, too, Winton rather hogging the business in the 1920s, no doubt because of their long-standing marine connections and also because their 100-hp-at-1000-rpm six-cylinder diesel fit so nicely into boats of the 40'-50' class: it only weighed around 2500 pounds. Buda connected with

> By the late 1920s, Cummins had become a visible entity in the yachting world. Speedway, Hall-Scott, Standard and Winton got into diesel, too...

MAN diesels from Germany; Mercedes-Benz sent over a few representatives; and Bessemer offered a 300-hp reversible diesel that weighed 30,000 pounds.

Diesel progress, of course, was long hampered by weight. The Bessemer weighed 100 pounds per hp; other manufacturers boasted if they could get the weight down to 25 pounds per hp in smaller engines. Thus, around 1925, "diesel cruiser" usually meant something like 100' LOA, twin-screw, and good for 16-18 knots. In 1929, Clessie L. Cummins, among the first to seriously attack the weight problem, put one of his 50-hp engines in a 1925 Packard sedan and drove it from Indianapolis to the New York Auto Show on $1.38 worth of fuel; but for the Depression, the feat would have gained wider notice and the diesel trend which is so often remarked upon today would have been underway long ago.

That a diesel would not collapse a Packard's suspension was notable enough, and the fuel economy more so. Indeed, as early as 1912, Yachting noted that if a boat were run 10 hours per day, the saving on diesel fuel at three cents per gallon, versus gasoline at nine cents per gallon, could amount to $1800 per year; knowing the times and its readership, Yachting pointed out that $1800 amounted to the interest on $36,000 at five percent, but did not comment on the probability of a pleasure yacht actually running 10 hours per day all year.

Remarking on diesel cruisers (of the 100' class) in Yachting for June, 1931, Reginald W. Cromly observed: "Fuel economy and a reduced fire hazard are the potent attractions of the Diesel engine...For economy over long distances, the Diesel motor is unchallengeable, but the gas engine is still supreme for high speed...the prevailing Diesel-mindedness seems sometimes to outweigh the fair merits of gas engines...The preference for Diesel motors is now frequently determined by a state of mind, without any technical considerations. The Diesel engine is in vogue."

Which is a fair assessment of the matter 50 years later.

DETROIT TRIUMPHANT

With grave profundity, dockside savants frequently aver that the marine business is "conservative" and slow to change. In fact, any industry that depends on expensive casting machinery and which requires considerable lead time to design not only the product but the system to produce the product, will be conservative. Once Winton or Kermath set up molds to cast engine blocks, they were not going to discard them until they had squeezed the last penny out of them; once Palmer or Lathrop set up to marinize engines from other suppliers, they were not going to change until the benefits would pay for the change. In the long run, the marine engine business would go to those who could stay closest to the leading edge of change. In the long run, that meant those who could afford change through economics of scale—in other words, the automobile industry.

As noted, the automobile industry was sniffing around the waterfront even before 1930. However, before 1930, the marine industry represented petty cash to the automobile people: up to the Depression, the automotive industry could sell anything with four wheels that could cough its way out of a dealership, so great was America's eagerness to be on the road. During the Depression, the industry couldn't afford to pursue marine business; during WWII it couldn't pursue it at all, although Chrysler sold many a Crown for navy launches and Detroit Diesel sold many, many of the 6-71 diesels, developed in 1938, for landing craft. After WWII, once again, the public would buy any car that would run, so Detroit had no reason to look at boats.

The relative slowdown began in the early 1950s, as evidenced by the mid-'fifties failure of such venerable firms as Packard, Hudson, and Nash, and by the inroads of foreign cars, which reached 10 percent of sales by 1957 (the year the Edsel came out). Given the slowdown, the automobile industry was amenable to a marine proposition as the 1950s dawned; more importantly, they had the goodies in the form of postwar V8 engines that developed up to 200 hp. So what if such engines had to be held down to 3500 rpm for longevity? They would give five good years at that speed. So what if 3500 rpm was too fast for a propeller? A reduction gear such as the new (1949) Paragon or Borg-Warner (1957) took care of high revs nicely.

The marine engine world after 1950, which really means after the Depression and WWII, somewhat resembled an elite suburb invaded by irreverent hippies. The dignified Establishment—Standard, Winton, Hall-Scott, Kermath, Sterling, Scripps—watched in horror as cheap, boisterous automotive V8's bearing all manner of marinizers' names invaded their turf. Who cared what forgotten race Sterling or Scripps had won in 1920? Ford, Cadillac, Oldsmobile, Mercury and Lincoln V8's were driving boats to higher speeds in the express-cruiser world of the 1950s and cost half as much. Those who couldn't afford a new, freshly-painted Interceptor (Ford) or Graymarine (American Motors) engine by the late 'fifties could pull one out of a wrecked car and bolt on an excellent marine kit from one of several marinizers. What did the Establishment do? With as much discretion and dignity as they could muster, they closed up shop or retired into convenient mergers. They haven't been heard from for nearly 30 years.

To their credit, from 1930 to 1950, marine engines exhibited more progressive engineering than automotive engines. New recruits such as Red Wing and Continental joined the fun, along with Universal, Lauson, Wisconsin, and others, including the diminutive Briggs and Stratton and the mighty Nordberg. Marine engines typically had larger crankshafts than automotive engines and had the best of dual-point ignition systems for a more-sustained spark under load.

> ...No matter where the engines came from or whose name they bore, the growth in diesel numbers showed the inexorable drift of the boating world to diesel power.

DIESELS TRIUMPHANT

The authentic change between 1930 and 1950, though, was the development of the diesel trend (an awful word—but it has been a trend). National-Superior invested effort in yacht installations, as did Waukesha, Caterpillar, Detroit Diesel, Atlas Imperial, not to mention the already-arrived Cummins and *mirabile dictu,* Mack, the trucks with the bulldog. Meanwhile, the old gasoline names—Kermath, Gray, Scripps, Palmer, Lathrop, et al.—developed their own diesels, often by putting their paint scheme and nameplate on someone else's engine, as Gray did with Perkins diesels. No matter where the engines came from or whose name they bore, the growth in diesel numbers showed the inexorable drift of the boating world to diesel power. As with gasoline engines, the diesel game would ultimately go to those with the production volume to keep prices down, and with dealership networks to keep engines running. Thus, of a dozen diesels prominent at the first big, post-WWII New York Boat Show in 1947, only a few remain, while the vacancies have been filled with foreign engines. Stated tautologically, the marine engine market belongs to those who can stay in it.

By now, despite the probity of Cromley's previously quoted remarks, gasoline power has become the also-ran. It has all but disappeared in sailboats, its last representative being the Universal Atomic Four. Inboard buyers still choose gasoline power for sound reasons of initial cost, but they all wish they could afford diesel engines.

Diesel itself has come a long way toward light weight, the common average being about 7½ pounds per hp (against about 4 pounds per gasoline hp in V8 lots), a reduction largely the product of the supercharger, which uses exhaust-gas pressure to drive a compressor that force-feeds the engine with air and allows it to burn more fuel, and generate more heat, than its size would otherwise allow. Here again, Cummins led the way with shaft-driven superchargers in the 1930s. WWII technology taught the escape from supercharging constraints via the turbocharger, and turbochargers are now standard on any diesel with yacht-club ambitions.

WHITHER HENCE?

To survey the past invites predictions about the future. Odds are that, for the next 20 years, things will stay much as they are. The market offers no growth sufficient to justify anyone tooling up to produce a new brand-name of engine. Indeed, any domestic scarcity is filled from overseas, and the foreign options have hardly been touched, much less exhausted. Hence, look for no new engine manufacturers to spring up; existing firms have the market well-covered and its rate of growth is declining.

The news in the next generation will be the application of electronics to engine monitoring and fuel injection. Sensors will read humidity, atmospheric pressure, air temperatures, rates of combustion, and exhaust gas composition, and they will meter fuel with the exactitude of a miser paying the servants. Such systems are in place on gasoline-powered automobiles, and American Bosch and others are developing similar systems for diesels.

Regarding all this, Herr Otto would wonder if his patents were being infringed, Herr Diesel would offer his enigmatic smile, and the boat owner of, say, 1910, would think all the fun—the rackety running, the seeping oil, the backfiring that could shatter a crankcase, the blowtorch pre-heating — had gone out of powerboating.

CORRESPONDENCE

Dear Editor:

The opinions of fine sailing yachts by your correspondents Fraser and Jean Fraser-Harris are held in high regard by myself and my wife.

We are very interested in the fine boats built by the Shannon Boat Company and would like to order your appraisal of the 38 foot ketch, if indeed one has been made. If no appraisal exists would you be kind enough to express your views as to the boat's quality for ocean crossing and liveaboard capabilities.
Dick and Carol Clark
Arlington, Virginia

Editor's Note: We have not yet done a survey of the Shannon 38, but this issue contains an extensive survey report on the Shannon 50. These survey reports are as much an evaluation of a boatbuilder's practices and philosophies as they are specific reports on a given boat, and you should find this one a thorough discussion of all of the Shannon Boat Company's work and workmanship.

Dear Editor:

I'm a new subscriber to *Nautical Quarterly* but am enjoying the issues immensely. Your survey pieces are really an educational insight into the boat/construction/usage, etc. field. I particularly am impressed with the Albin 43 and wrote to the company for additional data. My wife and I have enjoyed boats all of our married life, but I've never been able to get her enthusiastic over sail. She claimed when I took her along I only wanted some extra weight to hike out over the side! Thus we compromised on power (motor cruisers) and have had several up to 40 feet.

I've been attempting a further compromise for almost a year now since I saw an ad for a 40 ft. Stonington in a Sparkman & Stephens page in Yachting. We got most of the particulars and I traced down the builder, now retired; the yard is a condo, and he remembered building the boat in 1952 for a New Yorker, who is still the owner and now wants to sell. The boat is located on Long Island, and after refastening this previous winter the owner (82 years young) is using her for the season. The boat is diesel-powered (350 hp), one engine since installation in the early 60's, diesel generator, glass decks, otherwise pretty standard equipment. The price began at 50, went to 38, down to 26 and now is subject to offer.

I bring out these facts only for background; what I really would appreciate is some personal observations about a Stonington, since I note in NQ that your survey team, the Fraser-Harrises, had one for 2 years. Could you, if time permits, ask them to drop me a line with their thoughts on a Stonington.

Thanks ever so much and good luck with your survey feature... it's really good.
Don Larson
Baton Rouge, Louisiana

Dear Editor:

Recently I was reviewing the spring, 1982, issue of *Nautical Quarterly* (#17) when I came upon Peter Rogers's exciting painting "Winter, George's Bank." I was fascinated by the realism of this work and closely identified with the subject matter.

I've been assigned to the Narcotics Division of the Los Angeles Police Department for nearly twenty years. Last July I was working in an undercover operation, posing as a commercial fisherman. I had been hired by several individuals to off-load a mother ship three hundred miles off the California coast. Enroute to our rendezvous location we encountered a severe Pacific storm. After a day-long search, we located our ship, a 110′ trawler, loaded with 16 tons of Colombian marijuana. The vessel, sea condition, and a setting sun bore such a strong resemblance to this painting.

I've since obtained a copy of this *Nautical Quarterly* and have reviewed this painting on numerous occasions. Peter Rogers is obviously a man quite familiar with the sea and her beauty. I have admiration for his work.
Sergeant Fred S. McKnight
Los Angeles Police Department
Narcotics Division
Los Angeles, California

Dear Editor:

I loved Willard Bond's paintings in *Nautical Quarterly* 20 so much that I called the Sportsman's Edge Gallery to order prints they sell of two of the paintings shown in your article. I thought others doing so might like to know that Sportsman's Edge's address is 134 East 74th Street in New York, and not 76th St. as printed on page 61.
Christina Colbert
New York, New York

Dear Editor:

I was delighted to see your autumn issue of *Nautical Quarterly* (#19) and read the article about the Alburys. We have been visiting Man O'War Cay for over 25 years and built a house there 13 years ago. Mr. Emerson is our caretaker and good friend. Joe Albury was here visiting us last week, and we are the family who took him to Alaska and canoeing down the Yukon.
Marjorie Christiansen
Rocky River, Ohio

Dear Editor:

I had subscribed to *Nautical Quarterly* for my husband, Charles. I knew he would enjoy reading it. It is a beautiful magazine—and he has enjoyed every copy. (So have I.)

Of course Charles was thrilled over the article about Jack Hargrave in the 19th issue. You were a dear to be so complimentary of Charles, too. At 85 it is much appreciated. Nothing in his life gave him as much pleasure at the time, or now in retrospect, as the encouragement he could give to people if needed. As I have written before, the ones he has helped have always remembered it. One man calls him every Thanksgiving just to say "thank you." Incidentally, this man is a millionaire now. He had the ability and talent, but just needed the help at the right time.
Mrs. Charles F. Johnson
Port St. Lucie, Florida

Dear Editor:

Your recent article about Gar Wood was a real trip in nostalgia. Your writer Mr. Kevin Desmond covered a period when I spent a very large percent of my time on the Detroit River. Mr. Desmond is an excellent writer, but I wouldn't want him as a navigator. He said that Gar Wood's residence, Greyhaven, was near Algonac—a miss by about 30 miles. Greyhaven is almost directly across the Detroit River from the mentioned Detroit Yacht Club, a distance of about ¾ of a mile.

Many times in the early 'thirties we sailed an old Ludke catboat across the river to visit the old Grey Fox. His home contained never-ending mechanical wonders. Greyhaven is now a shambles, a truly sorry sight, a victim of vandalism—gone but not forgotten by a senior citizen who still sails the Detroit River and Lake St. Clair.

Nautical Quarterly is always welcome, especially in the winter with the lakes frozen over. It has been a yearly Christmas gift from my daughter who is convinced that after 51 years her father still enjoys sailing his own boat, a Tanzer 22.
George O. Young
Grosse Pointe, Michigan

---

1. TITLE OF PUBLICATION: NAUTICAL QUARTERLY. A. PUBLICATION NO.: 500-330.2. DATE OF FILING: SEPTEMBER 30, 1982 3. FREQUENCY OF ISSUE: QUARTERLY (SPRING, SUMMER, FALL, WINTER). A. NO. OF ISSUES PUBLISHED ANNUALLY: 4. B. ANNUAL SUBSCRIPTION PRICE: $49.50. 4. LOCATION OF KNOWN OFFICE OF PUBLICATION (STREET, CITY, STATE AND ZIP CODE) (NOT PRINTERS): 373 PARK AVENUE SOUTH, NEW YORK, MANHATTAN COUNTY, NY 10016. 5. LOCATION OF THE HEADQUARTERS OF GENERAL BUSINESS OFFICES OF THE PUBLISHERS (NOT PRINTERS): 373 PARK AVENUE SOUTH, NEW YORK, NY 10016. 6. NAMES AND COMPLETE ADDRESSES OF PUBLISHER, EDITOR, AND MANAGING EDITOR: PUBLISHER (NAME AND ADDRESS): DONALD C. MCGRAW, JR., 373 PARK AVENUE SOUTH, NEW YORK, NY 10016; EDITOR (NAME AND ADDRESS): JOSEPH GRIBBINS, 373 PARK AVENUE SOUTH, NEW YORK, NY 10016; MANAGING EDITOR (NAME AND ADDRESS) MICHAEL LEVITT, 373 PARK AVENUE SOUTH, NEW YORK, NY 10016. 7. OWNER (IF OWNED BY A CORPORATION, ITS NAME AND ADDRESS MUST BE STATED AND ALSO IMMEDIATELY THEREUNDER THE NAMES AND ADDRESS OF STOCKHOLDERS OWNING OR HOLDING 1 PERCENT OR MORE OF TOTAL AMOUNT OF STOCK. IF NOT OWNED BY A CORPORATION, THE NAMES AND ADDRESSES OF INDIVIDUAL OWNERS MUST BE GIVEN. IF OWNED BY A PARTNERSHIP OR OTHER UNINCORPORATED FIRM, ITS NAME AND ADDRESS, AS WELL AS THAT OF EACH INDIVIDUAL, MUST BE GIVEN. IF THE PUBLICATION IS PUBLISHED BY A NON-PROFIT ORGANIZATION, ITS NAME AND ADDRESS MUST BE STATED.): NAUTICAL QUARTERLY, CO.., 373 PARK AVENUE SOUTH, NEW YORK, NY 10016; DONALD C. MCGRAW, JR., 373 PARK AVENUE SOUTH, NEW YORK, NY 10016; JOSEPH GRIBBINS, 373 PARK AVENUE SOUTH, NEW YORK, NY 10016; B. MARTIN PEDERSEN, 373 PARK AVENUE SOUTH, NEW YORK, NY 10016; C.S. LOVELACE, 373 PARK AVENUE SOUTH, NEW YORK, NY 10016. 8. KNOWN BONDHOLDERS, MORTGAGES, AND OTHER SECURITY HOLDERS OWNING OR HOLDING 1 PERCENT OR MORE OF TOTAL AMOUNT OF BONDS, MORTGAGES OR OTHER SECURITIES (IF THERE ARE NONE, SO STATE): NONE. 9. FOR COMPLETION BY NONPROFIT ORGANIZATIONS AUTHORIZED TO MAIL AT SPECIAL RATES: NOT APPLICABLE. 10. EXTENT AND NATURE OF CIRCULATION: A. TOTAL NO. OF COPIES PRINTED (NET PRESS RUN)—AVERAGE NO. OF COPIES EACH ISSUE DURING PRECEDING 12 MONTHS: 19,159; ACTUAL NO. OF COPIES OF SINGLE ISSUE PUBLISHED NEAREST TO FILING DATE: 21,220. B. PAID CIRCULATION (1.) SALES THROUGH DEALERS AND CARRIERS, STREET VENDORS AND COUNTER SALES—AVERAGE NO. OF COPIES EACH ISSUE DURING PRECEDING 12 MONTHS: 1,410; ACTUAL NO. OF

CORRESPONDENCE

Dear Editor:

I worked for Gar Wood in 1943 on the design and construction of the Bomb Target Boat. There are some errors in the text in the article on Gar Wood by Kevin Desmond in *Nautical Quarterly* 20. There was steel armor plate only over the engine and fuel-tank compartment. Planes were never considered for the deck, which was of half-inch 5-ply gum plywood. Her original power was a pair of Allison W-3420s, burning gasoline, of about 2000 hp each. These drove the twin-screw propeller system of the 110′ PC boats used by the Navy. All was remote radio-controlled. She was a very interesting craft on which to work, more interesting at sea. And Gar Wood was the most interesting of all!

David D. Beach, Manager
Engineering Services
National Marine Manufacturers Association
Chicago, Illinois

Dear Editor:

This is the first and only time I have felt the need to write a complimentary letter to a publisher!

As an original subscriber, with all the issues received, and stored safely but within arms reach, and upon receipt of my 20th volume, I must tell you and your staff down to the very last person who completes the task of mailing...Bravo!...and Kudos! I cannot tell you how much I truly enjoy your efforts—the quality, the efficiency, and the variety of related boat articles with their very excellent photos and artwork.

Not since I was a small child with the adventures of Tom Swift and his runabout have I been able to enjoy such secret wishes and fantasies about boats as I do with your books. As a thrice-time sailboat owner, and now a 180° powerboat owner, I still experience the thrill of sail combined with the craftmanship of the makers, along with the joy of the powerboats and their varied uses and styles.

Please accept my sincere thanks for the continuity of your excellence, and my wishes to you and your staff for a long and successful publication.

Ted Nettler
South Pasadena, California

Dear Editor:

Please tell me the breed of dog depicted on page 70 of *Nautical Quarterly* 19, and where one can be obtained.

Carter E. Duncan
Le Roy, Illinois

Editor's Note: Bruce Kirby's dog, Leroy Brown, is a Chesapeake Bay Retriever, named after your home town, and available wherever Chesapeake Bay dogs are sold.

Dear Editor:

Recently while going over *Nautical Quarterly* 15, I read the correspondence concerning the strong language in the story "Arster Drudgin'" by Randall Peffer. I did think at the time that the foul language printed was unnecessary. You understand that I have been exposed to some champions in this field and have at times given a good performance myself when I thought it appropriate. It is my experience, however, that such use of language by dredge boatmen is very much the exception rather than the rule as is suggested by Peffer. After reading "Arster Drudgin'" a reader not familiar with the subject would get the impression that the standard dredge boatman is foul and his boat is a "floating junkyard."

I assure you that this is not the case. At a recent race for the skipjacks during Chesapeake Appreciation Days, most all the vessels appeared like fine yachts. The notable exception was the *Ruby G. Ford* that was in your story. Even during the working season, the standard of cleanliness is generally excellent. But, that is another story.

The quality of material in *Nautical Quarterly* is, of course, excellent.

Frederick E. Hecklinger
Annapolis, Maryland

Dear Editor:

I personally thoroughly enjoyed Skip Novak's two accounts of the past Whitbread Race. They refreshed my memory and allowed me a few moments to relive the race. I might comment on Neil Bergt's and Mike Farley's letters critical of Skip's articles. The past Whitbread was not Skip's first long ocean race. He's a professional and has always been held in the highest regard by those who've sailed with and under him. I crewed with him in the 1979 Parmelia Race and the whole crew parted ways close friends after 13,000 miles thanks to Skip's leadership. His fellow crewmates aboard *King's Legend* in the '77-'78 Whitbread, I'm sure, felt the same about him. I feel that Bergt's and Farley's comments should be directed to themselves and not Skip.

Brian Hancock
Watch Captain
Alaska Eagle *Campaign*

Dear Editor:

Having just read the "Amaretto" article by Joe Upton in issue #20, it is one of the best descriptions of near-terror that can develop during night fishing in places that should be avoided even in daylight. Gives we rip-trollers pause.

The author and you, both, deserve a bow for an exceptional piece.

Neil C. Lindeman
St. Michaels, Maryland

Dear Editor:

As a new subscriber I was pleased to receive my first issue, *Nautical Quarterly* 19. Having seen several previous issues, I am happy to say that I am not disappointed.

As I have spent the better part of my eighty years "messing around in boats," I have been imbued with the emphasis on the word "proper." The old-timers who contributed so much to my dedicated interest in boats and boating taught me to respect the proper handling of lines, rigging, tying of knots and all the other functions one must perform in seamanship. Therefore it was with some surprise that I examined the lower photograph on page 54 of the issue. Both of the Flemish coils of the bow lines are improperly turned. As the lines are right-laid the coils should be made up in a clock-wise fashion. Also, a look at the belaying of those lines fills me with consternation. The line on the port cleat is belayed with a final half-hitch in the wrong direction. The line on the starboard cleat is made into a rats nest which defies other analysis.

I can only hope that Jim Donovan did not belay and finish off those mooring lines himself. I can forgive the photographer as a probable landlubber, but the picture editor...?

Small criticism of an otherwise excellent publication. I look forward to further issues with great anticipation. Note that I am including an order for two back issues herewith.

Burton Dezendorf
Pine Beach, New Jersey

Dear Editor:

I was previously the first mate on the Hatteras yacht *Hatterascal* which was featured in *Nautical Quarterly* 19. Until recently I had not seen the issue and was more than impressed with it. The *Hatterascal* had been photographed in the past but *Nautical Quarterly* has done the finest job of them all. Congratulations on a job well done.

David McCormick
Fort Lauderdale, Florida

COPIES OF SINGLE ISSUE PUBLISHED NEAREST TO FILING DATE: 1,875; (2.) MAIL SUBSCRIPTIONS— AVERAGE NO. OF COPIES EACH ISSUE DURING PRECEDING 12 MONTHS: 16,797; ACTUAL NO. OF COPIES OF SINGLE ISSUE PUBLISHED NEAREST TO FILING DATE: 17,945; C. TOTAL PAID CIRCULATION (SUM OF 10B1 AND 10B2)— AVERAGE NO. OF COPIES EACH ISSUE DURING PRECEDING 12 MONTHS: 18,207; ACTUAL NO. OF COPIES OF SINGLE ISSUE PUBLISHED NEAREST TO FILING DATE: 19,820; D. FREE DISTRIBUTION BY MAIL, CARRIER OR OTHER MEANS, SAMPLES, COMPLIMENTARY, AND OTHER FREE SAMPLES— AVERAGE NO. OF COPIES EACH ISSUE DURING PRECEDING 12 MONTHS: 388; ACTUAL NO. OF COPIES OF SINGLE ISSUE PUBLISHED NEAREST TO FILING DATE: 431; E. TOTAL DISTRIBUTION (SUM OF C AND D)—AVERAGE NO. OF COPIES EACH ISSUE DURING PRECEDING 12 MONTHS: 18,595; ACTUAL NO. OF COPIES OF SINGLE ISSUE PUBLISHED NEAREST TO FILING DATE: 20,251; F. COPIES NOT DISTRIBUTED (1.) OFFICE USE, LEFT OVER, UNACCOUNTED. SPOILED AFTER PRINTING— AVERAGE NO. OF COPIES EACH ISSUE DURING PRECEDING 12 MONTHS: 564; ACTUAL NO. OF COPIES OF SINGLE ISSUE PUBLISHED NEAREST TO FILING DATE: 969; (2.) RETURNS FROM NEWS AGENTS— AVERAGE NO. OF COPIES EACH ISSUE DURING PRECEDING 12 MONTHS: 0; ACTUAL NO. OF COPIES OF SINGLE ISSUE PUBLISHED NEAREST TO FILING DATE: 0; G. TOTAL (SUM OF E, F1 AND 2—SHOULD EQUAL NET PRESS RUN SHOWN IN A)— AVERAGE NO. OF COPIES EACH ISSUE DURING PRECEDING 12 MONTHS: 19,159; ACTUAL NO. OF COPIES OF SINGLE ISSUE PUBLISHED NEAREST TO FILING DATE: 21,220. 11. I CERTIFY THAT THE STATEMENTS MADE BY ME ABOVE ARE CORRECT AND COMPLETE (SIGNATURE AND TITLE OF EDITOR, PUBLISHER, BUSINESS MANAGER, OR OWNER): DAVID B. WALLACE, CIRCULATION DIRECTOR. 12. FOR COMPLETION BY PUBLISHERS MAILING AT THE REGULAR RATES (SECTION 132.121, POSTAL SERVICE MANUAL): 39 U.S.C. 3626 PROVIDES IN PERTINENT PART "NO PERSON WHO WOULD HAVE BEEN ENTITLED TO MAIL MATTER UNDER FORMER SECTION 4359 OF THIS TITLE SHALL MAIL SUCH MATTER AT THE RATES PROVIDED UNDER THIS SUBSECTION UNLESS HE FILES ANNUALLY WITH THE POSTAL SERVICE A WRITTEN REQUEST FOR PERMISSION TO MAIL MATTER AT SUCH RATES." IN ACCORDANCE WITH THE PROVISIONS OF THIS STATUTE, I HEREBY REQUEST PERMISSION TO MAIL THE PUBLICATION NAMED IN ITEM 1 AT THE PHASED POSTAGE RATES AUTHORIZED BY 39 U.S.C. 3626. (SIGNATURE AND TITLE OF EDITOR, PUBLISHER, BUSINESS MANAGER, OR OWNER): DAVID B. WALLACE, CIRCULATION DIRECTOR.

CREDITS

Cover:	Benjamin Mendlowitz	**44:**	Courtsey of Bermuda News Bureau	**70:**	Allan Weitz (top right) Benjamin Mendlowitz (top left and bottom)	**101:**	Robert Foley
2-4:	Stanley Rosenfeld					**102-105:**	Photos by Jim Brown Drawings courtesy of Nauticat, Inc.
5:	Courtesy of Cantieri Riva	**46:**	Courtesy of Arthur Knapp, Jr.				
6:	Courtesy of G no Gervasoni	**47:**	Dan Nerney	**71:**	Benjamin Mendlowitz (right) Allan Weitz (left)		
8-10:	Stanley Rosenfeld	**48-57:**	Jim Brown			**106:**	Photographs by Rob McCready
13-17:	Courtesy of Cantieri Riva	**58 & 59:**	Benjamin Mendlowitz	**72-79:**	Benjamin Mendlowitz		
18-29:	Dan Nerney	**61 & 63 & 65:**	Drawings courtesy of Philip C. Bolger	**80 & 85 & 86:**	Illustrations by Gary Kelley	**120:**	Courtesy of Harwill, Inc.
30:	Courtesy of Arthur Knapp, Jr.			**90-95:**	Peter Neumann		
31:	Roger Shope	**67:**	Benjamin Mendlowitz	**98:**	Robert Foley		Nautical Quarterly is printed by Federated Lithographers, Inc. Providence, Rhode Island.
32-37:	Courtesy of Arthur Knapp, Jr.			**99:**	Photo by Robert Foley Drawing courtesy of Shannon Boat Co.		
38-40:	Morris Rosenfeld						
42:	Fred E. Hahnel